Threaded Journeys

Casting a fly, roaming the woods, learning by doing and wanting more…

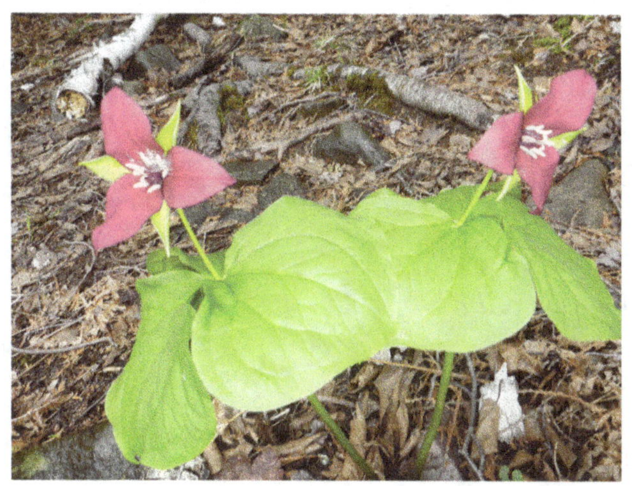

By

Tom Johnson

Sutton Press
Sutton, Massachusetts
2016

Library of Congress Cataloging-in-Publication Data
ISBN 978-0-692-60259-1

First Edition

Poems:

"Lure" by Karin Johnson p. 79

"The Quest" by Jerry Johnson p.102

"Who Belongs" by Tom Johnson p. 133

Threaded Journeys

Fishing, Hunting, Conservation, Adventure…and Our Future

Table of Contents

Author: Tom Johnson

Website: www.tomjohnsononline.com

For: Pam, Katie, Karin, Bethany

Edited by Karin Johnson & Katie Johnson

~Foreword

When we peer at life in all its essence, meaning and mystery, how do we perceive it? In turn, how do we live it? As we travel through time we learn, adapt and change through the many life experiences that embrace and challenge us. We use discernment to help with our decisions, to employ ideas, and to provide security and a sense of well-being. Acquired knowledge and perceptions should be used to our advantage, but I have learned that we must be open and ready for new interpretations and modifications. I have also found that living and feeling comfortable with ourselves and our environment requires a satisfaction that is not stagnant or totally fulfilled. There are multiple insights, mores and values that help grant us stability in an unstable world and, for me, journeying on the cutting edge of life with body, mind and spirit makes life much more meaningful, lively and fulfilling. In my passage I require a venerable mix of interests that merge family, business, conservation and sporting pursuits that are shared with others, and a desire to make a difference. Much of this adventure leaves me vulnerable and at risk. It is natural that we desire to guard ourselves from harm and from making untimely and inappropriate decisions, but it is always wise to leave ourselves somewhat exposed and susceptible to the unknown and the mysterious. It is necessary to do what we can to correct wrongs where we see them and to share the positives in order to strengthen and enhance them. We do ourselves a disservice when we do not uncover and promote corrective actions to calamities that have a direct bearing on our quality of life. Often we think someone else will catch the error and correct it, but many blunders continue unabated and often become irreversible over time. There is a good reason why the statement 'nipping it in the bud' was made. In the sportsman's world much progress has been made, but there are still multiple problems and mismanagements that cry out to be uncovered, exposed and corrected.

Life will always have a knack for building us up and breaking us down. How we ultimately handle and look at our situation will determine our successes or failures. Only we can determine the outcome. Some of the world's greatest successes emerged from the ashes of defeat and loss. Many people do their best when their backs are against the wall, when life circumstances place them in precarious and challenging positions. The world may have its opinion, but it is only your attitude, faith and action that ultimately count in the game of living. Actively-engaged pragmatic people who envision a better tomorrow and work to renew it, is what the world needs more of to help insure a safer, more productive and content society. Part of our jobs should be building people up, regardless of their success or failure — not breaking them down as we often witness with the media and society at large. Governments should help facilitate our quest for 'freedom, liberty and the pursuit of happiness', rather than stagnate our existence with overburdening debt, misguided policies and politically-motivated oppressive taxes, regulations and laws.

The natural world beckons me and many others with its beauty and uncompromising wonders. Although it holds secrets that have been kept concealed since our planet was created, the exposed, raw nakedness of our earth leaves much for us to explore and encompass. Its natural resources are ample and plenty. Many of the earth's assets have and will continue to provide fuel, heat and comfort to a growing population. New technologies will enable us to utilize them more safely, with less earth and sea degradation. For our security and well-being, becoming energy independent and less reliant on foreign sources is of critical importance. It will always be necessary to have a deep respect for what we garner from the earth's surface, sub-soils, rivers and oceans. In the process of exploration and employment, we must prevent undue damage to our landscapes, waterways and fragile aquatic life. Sensibly applied environmental laws and procedures are essential and smart to use for the short term and for the preservation of the earth's ecosystems for future generations to enjoy.

The forward chapters propel us into a sportsman's world — an uncompromising natural world that promises only two things: success and disappointment. More often it is the combination of the two that is the reality, and much can be learned and applied when setbacks take a toll on us. Sportsmen tend to have a unique lens on life. They recognize necessary laws and initiatives for conserving and preserving our wildlife and environments and support these actions with their dollars. They also enjoy the fishing and hunting that go hand-in-hand with this outdoor package. The true sportsman accepts rigid, unbending circumstances as he pries his way fly casting downstream or as he sweats to a mountain peak in quest of ridge-running game. He counts his blessings each and every day, for within these mysteries of life and for what he sees before him, he recognizes that he was made for a purpose and that his life is ultimately in God's hands. In his journey he must seek and find that "inner peace that passes all understanding." For some of this harmony he can find it by surrounding himself in the earth's wonderland.

This is a different kind of sportsman's book with interlaced tangents and diversities not often found with fishing and hunting adventure narratives. First and foremost, sharing these outdoor ventures is what moves me. It is my hope that this reading proves engaging and will help spur readers to go afield and enjoy the splendors that natural, wild surroundings provide. However, there are a multiple number of convergent issues including health, welfare and policy considerations that have a direct bearing upon sportsman and our national well-being. It is my desire to discuss some of these concerns together and to do our part to rectify problems rather than to settle with the dire consequences of inaction. We are cast into a world that is composed of a complex mix of private and government entities. Within this multifaceted package, special interests and politically motivated actions constantly sweep into our view. We witness the push and pull, the give and take, the logical and irrational of human behavior, and eventual policies that are written into law.

The ultimate sporting challenge will be using whatever influence we can muster to help preserve natural landscapes, waterways and the native fish and wildlife that inhabit these places, while mitigating and facilitating directives that provide us with necessary goods and services.

At this moment I would have preferred to be casting my fly line out and over an emerald-blue wild river pool with the eternal hope that the splendid silver salmon or earth-toned speckled trout would oblige my feeble offering, peel off some line and go airborne. But, to a lessening degree of enthusiasm, I put pen to paper, and even with the desired pull to pry me from this task, something deep inside spurs me forward — and inscribe I must…

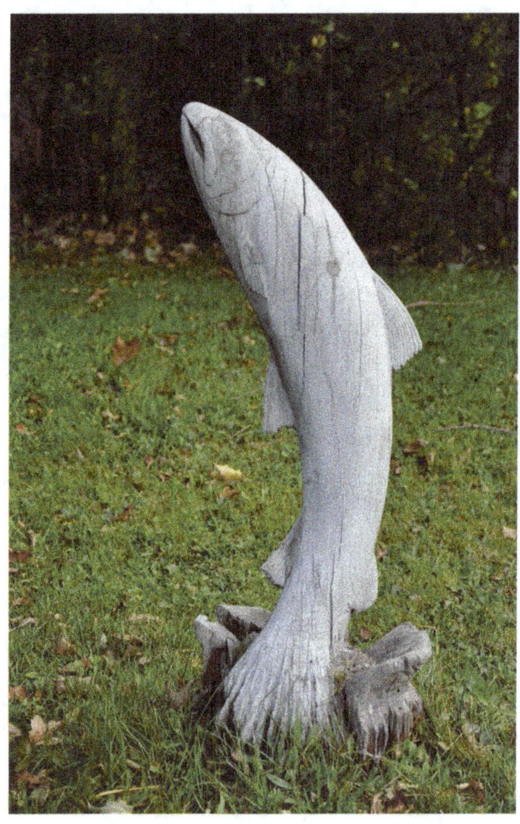

Chapter 1

Blue-Green Planet

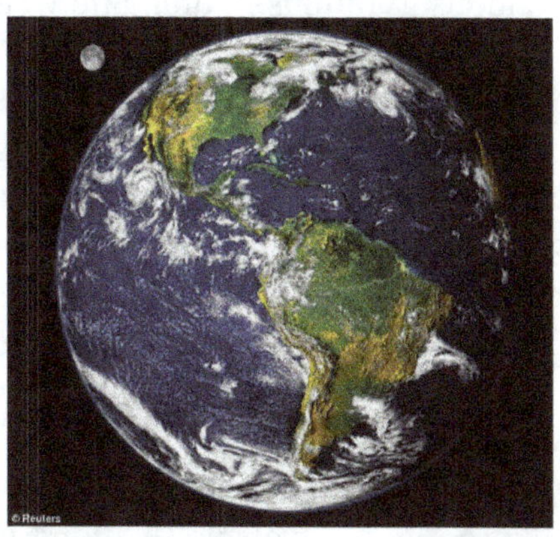

It is estimated that the earth is 4.54 billion years old. The beyond-our-comprehension dynamics of this time span puts us in a position of awe and wonder as we ponder, study and come to at least some minute understanding of our foundation and place in the universe. The world has been listening to and dissecting alarms that portray human beings as major culprits in the demise of our planet, and that we have been negligent and wasteful as global warming initiators. Of course our presence over the last 200 years spanning the Industrial Age has certainly impacted the environment in negative ways with coal burning acid residues, over fishing the oceans, fracking practices to excrete oil and gas and piling our junk into dump mountains. It is my summation that we all have a responsibility to do our part to lessen true pollutants and to support conservation initiatives that make sense to educated, logical, common sense thinkers. It is my supportive belief, however, that the crucial and most critical internal and external changes to the earth are primarily natural occurrences that have been forged since the beginnings of our tiny planet. The earth is and has never been at a standstill. As it spins and revolves around the sun in its distinctive orbit, and as it continues to exude and prompt violent volcanoes, earthquakes, tsunamis and tornadoes, our planet is never at rest. As such, climatic change has always been a natural phenomenon. The earth or certain sectors of it may be in a warming trend that will change the face of the globe into the next century and beyond. But, much of this talk is conjecture and not necessarily fact. Regardless, carbon dioxide (CO2) is not our enemy and it is not a pollutant. It is an odorless, colorless gas that is a natural and necessary component of the biosphere. As we inhale oxygen, we exhale high concentrations of CO2. Plants and animals evolved on our planet when CO2 concentrations were approximately ten times larger than they are today. It seems that the earth did all right by itself producing, organizing and distributing high levels of carbon and its emissions over the course of many millennia. Some scientists are looking at the potentials of 50 to 100 year weather models which show some indication that the earth may be warming. I prefer to look at the natural model swings than span tens of thousands of years where we clearly see the earth's tremendous gyrations in dramatic weather occurrences.

   Ninety-Five percent of the earth's CO2 evolves from the natural occurrence of water vapor formation. Solar activity combined with the complex array of ocean currents which distribute heat and control weather systems are the primary drivers of climate change. We know from scientific studies including earth core samples that much of our northern hemisphere was ice-free during the last interglacial period 125,000 years ago. The climate was approximately 5 degrees warmer than the interglacial period we live in today. Historical Greenland was green, covered with conifer trees in a relatively mild climate. Antarctica has 90 % of the Earth's ice and ice formation is up over 40% since 1980. Arctic ice is down less than 7 %. These statistics are located in the NOAA GISS website (Nation Snow and Ice Data Center), University of Colorado. The U.S. National Climate Data Center states that the world in 2006 was only .03 degrees Celsius warmer than it was in 2001. When using unaltered historical NOAA/NASA data, there has been no true warming trend in the last 130 years.

   I assume that most people born 50 or more years ago don't remember the hysteria about the global cooling trend that was being highly expounded upon. During the 1970s the media endorsed global cooling alarmism with the dire threats of a new ice age. The reason for this cooling trend was the same reasoning used today in the media to describe global warming—human induced pollution. In an April 28, 1975 Newsweek article titled "The Cooling World", it was argued that global temperatures were falling and that a terrible calamity lay ahead. Our misfortune would include a drastic fall in food production with the resulting catastrophic results of a world-wide famine. *Time* magazine's 1977 cover showed a penguin on top of an ice pile with the words "How To Survive The Coming Ice Age." These articles and many others would never have been written without the general scientific community being in agreement that climate cooling was a real and threatening reality. Isn't it interesting to note that our general media today hasn't reminded us of these past beliefs which turned into fallacy. In lieu of this past behavior, should we question the current mania centered on global warming? Are the political and scientific blind again leading the blind? Although we now have better tools to predict weather trends and fluctuations short term, we are far from coming to absolute, uncontested reasons for the earth's ongoing, future shifting conditions. Governments and many environmental groups are using falsehoods to perpetuate myths about the threats of global warming. Their prime agenda includes promoting and having taxpayers pay for subsidies to prop up use for alternative energy sources such as solar and wind power, while demonizing the use of fossils fuels such as coal and oil. Little is mentioned regarding nuclear power as a reliable, basic pollutant-free source of energy which gives a big bang for the buck. I like the idea and growth of alternative energies as a component of the free enterprise system. Having at our disposal many energy choices can only be a good thing. But, promoting and spending tax payer dollars in this mix to promote myths about global warming is a huge disservice to the American public and the world at large.

It is probable that Atlantic salmon have been around for 60 million years. They have adapted and survived all of the earth's major climatic shifts including the last ice age glacial surge 10 thousand years ago. Salmon require cold, clean rivers and they may, over time, exit rivers that become too polluted or warm. Surely, as they have demonstrated over the millennia, their noses and instincts will find other rivers to migrate to and continue the life cycle of their species. The severity of global heat and cold transformations will often dictate which species continue to exist and which ones pass into history. Dinosaurs were lost, but other forms of life emerged. Science is still uncovering new species on earth and in the deep seas — some of which were undoubtedly created in response to climatic change over the millennia.

We seldom look at our lives and the impact we collectively have on our planet as we go about our daily business. Our concerns center on those parameters that help secure our health and welfare — namely work, shelter, food, transportation, recreation and social networks. If we can visualize earth from an outer space perspective and begin to focus more intently as we are propelled closer, we quickly witness before us a blue ocean ball linked between greener hues and whimsical windblown, cloud-covered atmospheres. Over the earth's crust we see the flowing pulse of river veins interlaced north, south, east and west with many emptying their life-nourishing provisions along their banks and into outstretched seas. Oceans cover 70% of the world's surface. They were and are the foundation of all life. Their most vital function is to regulate our climate, manufacture oxygen, remove carbon dioxide and purify the atmosphere. Their deep currents, dense in salt and algae, play a crucial role in the massive transportation of energy and food to the countless thousands of living organisms that inhabit its depths. The interplaying water ecosystems parlayed between the vast continents are varied and complex, and we are still in our infancy of understanding the connections that make these natural physical and chemical interactions vital to life on Earth. For those who don't believe in miracles, may I suggest that we are living on one of the Universes great miracles. The problem we all share is that we often don't sufficiently appreciate the view, the promise and the wonderment of this planet we call home. Many of us are ecologically illiterate and fail to collectively engage in correcting past ills and righting today's misdeeds that jeopardize our existence and sense of well-being.

As a sportsman, and concerned citizen I worry about the quality of life for all mankind as we enter the 21st century. We have an ongoing battle between 'environmentalists' who want to preserve everything and developers who desire to meet the public demand for goods by farming the earth's abundance of natural resources. I am a proponent of the free enterprise system and for the extraction of mineral deposits and other resources from the earth's crust and ocean depths. The houses we live in, the cars we drive, the food we eat, the clothes we wear, all come completely from or are derivatives of substances and composites originating from the natural world. Where there are corporeal needs, free enterprise has a knack of stepping forward and satisfying them. If, however, these resources are not sustainable or if the environment and its living inhabitants are threatened beyond reproach, developments must be curtailed or stopped altogether. Business can be a two-edged stone. Capital dollar formation with the open and free trade of goods and services are the mainstay of healthy economies and peoples worldwide. However, there is a big difference between businesses that make their living off the land and sea and those that don't. Natural resources are meant to be owned and shared by everyone, and hence they should be safeguarded and monitored to benefit the general population. As our world population grows, there is a mounting demand for fish, water, wood, minerals, coal, oil, gas, and other energy, shelter, and food resources. These realities will spur speculators to push the envelope of expansion into new territories with profit being a major incentive. While profit is necessary for businesses to exist and grow, equal focus needs to be measured towards safely guarding the environment where additional economic benefits can be gained for local economies. Sustainability is often a word that is misunderstood, distorted and overstated. A measurable example of sustainability that has worked well can be found in the lobster industry. By law all lobsters under a certain size and all females carrying eggs must be released back to the oceans after they are trapped. These simple practices along with daily quotas help insure the future vitality of the industry, while maintaining healthy populations of these historic crustaceans. Conservation's crying word for maintaining what is perceived as a working compromise between consumption and preservation has its place of promise, and some sustainable acts and measures do live up to their pledges to save species and ecosystems.

Fresh Waters

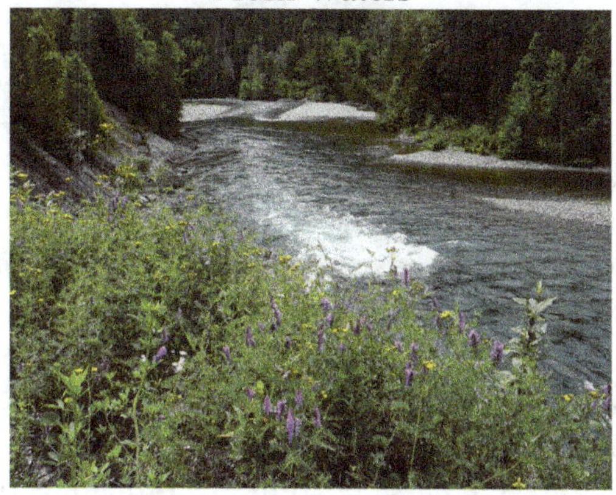

Going forward with actual facts in hand, probably the most important environmental concern and focus should be centered on our dwindling clean water supplies. This alert is particularly crucial in the agricultural food belt regions worldwide where aquifer ground waters from top to lower levels are being depleted at alarming rates to satisfy an ever growing human population. Seventy percent of the world's fresh water is used by agriculture, 20% by industry, 10% for municipal consumption. Many of the world's major rivers have experienced drastic depletions. Satellite images are revealing hard core evidence of severe ground water reduction in all the key agricultural centers around the globe, including the California farm belt that contributes over 10% of its produce to American consumers. As the water aquifers are being drained by deep well drilling, the upper land crust is sinking into the earth. Since more water is being extracted faster than aquifers can recover, we are facing a potentially catastrophic ending unless solutions are found. It would appear from this observer that we must find economically feasible ways to create fresh water from our oceans and seas to feed our needs to sustain agriculture, industry and to provide fresh water for drinking and hygiene. The desalination process whereby sea water is filtered through gravel and sand filters and then exposed to a reverse osmosis membrane system to remove the salt has been the only answer to this problem to date. Several plants are on line and planned along the California coast. It is a very costly process requiring the use of much electricity, and poses a number of environmental concerns, including where to put the salt once it's extracted. It is hoped that science will help to advance this technology to lower costs and to have operational systems that are less likely to harm the environment.

As a sportsman I am equally concerned for the many life forms that are created by having clean, healthy flowing rivers. Our native trout, salmon, bass and other species require well oxygenated waters to survive and provide recreational opportunities for millions of outdoor enthusiasts. Governments must wake up to this pending problem and work with industry and science to help create solutions. The time to act is now.

Fracking

The hydraulic fracturing (fracking) technique has expanded over the past few years to extract oil and gas from dense layers of rock far underneath the earth's surface. The procedure involves blasting water, chemicals and sand underground to break apart hardened substrate structures. How can this deadly carcinogenic mix of chemicals be safely stored once it is used up in the process of extracting? The problem is compounded when deep earthen-driven pipes extracting this liquid begin to leak. Concentrations of this toxic residue have found their way into streams, rivers and our water wells. Fish conservation organizations such as Trout Unlimited were up in arms after monitoring rivers with high concentrations of toxins and dying fish. State officials in Pennsylvania stopped these companies from using 'treatment plants' since the facilities were not adequately removing contaminants before releasing them into waterways. It was mandated that this liquid waste be deposited into 'injection wells', which the natural gas industry contends is the safest way of guarding the toxins. But, what is really safe? What happens to this deadly liquid mixture in these so-called injection wells over the millennia? Furthermore, several of these fracking sights have been at least temporarily closed due to the possibility that they have initiated earthquakes. Increasing seismic activity cannot be a good thing in anybody's backyard, particularly if this shifting of the earth's crust has the potential of exuding uncontained oil or gas into the neighboring mountains, valleys and waterways.

It would make much more sense to expand our initiatives in traditional energy production with tried, proven, and economically feasible methods, coupled with tighter safety procedures. Adding oil pipeline connections from Canada and re-energizing some nuclear power plants makes complete sense as part of our energy policy if economically feasible. It is critical, however, that these expansions are accomplished with the greatest care and concern for the environment. No technology is totally infallible. With over 2.5 million miles of pipelines in the U.S., there are going to be occasional oil, and gas spills. To keep these spills at a minimum, it is necessary to monitor the old sites with inspections and especially important to doubly insulate existing and new pipes from leaking where they cross and intersect rivers, ponds and lakes. It is always best to let the free markets handle our energy needs, and in that way only legitimately financed companies including alternative solar and wind production facilities will exist based on consumer demand. Markets exist, grow and fall based on consumer needs and requirements, not government mandates. A country cannot implement energy initiatives that the public doesn't want and won't support, unless it wants to throw away hard-earned taxpayer dollars. Although our state and federal governments play a crucial role in setting standards and procedures, our economy falters if energy policies are over regulated, and worse when needed energy growth is held hostage to political shenanigans and falsehoods. Alternative energy sources will emerge and grow. However, it may be decades before we may see the results in Europe where 10% of their energy needs are provided by solar, wind and geothermal sources. At issue here and most often overlooked by environmentalists who should be concerned, are the huge amounts of land and resources that are required to produce wind, solar and biofuel power. The uprooted, impaired land masses and visual pollutants that would emerge based on feeding and providing energy to a rising population would prove catastrophic and destructive to our environment. It is all about density. Where can we get the biggest bang for our buck with the smallest impact on land? Biofuels have low 'power densities' which refers to the amount of energy that can be received from a given volume, mass or area. It is estimated that the power density of corn ethanol is as low as .05 watts per square meter of farmland. The costs far outweigh the paybacks. In contrast, an average natural gas well that produces 60,000 cubic feet of gas a day has a power density of 28 watts per square meter. To replace one-tenth of U.S. oil use with biofuel switch grass would require the cultivation of about 37 million acres of land — an area about the size of Indiana. That proposal would be preposterous and nonsensical. Wind turbines have a power density of approximately 1 watt per square meter. New York City derives about 30% of its energy from two nuclear power plants which are located on 250 acres. If the city decided to convert to wind power, they would need to invest in about 760 square miles of land covered with wind turbines (an area just a bit smaller than Rhode Island) to capture this same percentage of energy need. This also negates the idea of a large-scale solar farm that would prove ineffective, costly to implement, maintain and to remove once its life span had lapsed. In 31 U.S. states there are currently 104 nuclear reactors providing 19.6% of our electricity. The reactors exude no pollutant emissions and have energy outputs that range between 478 megawatts to 1317 megawatts per station. Although the radioactive waste is toxic and long-lived, it can be stored safely in a much smaller container area in comparison to the waste produced from many other energy sources. Since their inception, nuclear power plants have only produced about 65,000 tons of toxic waste, which would cover an area approximately the size of a football field to a depth of 20 ft. In contrast, coal power plants in the U.S. produce about 130 million tons of coal ash in one single year. True environmentalists who love the word 'green' should be advocating the establishment of additional nuclear plants due to these low impact, low density and low pollutant factors.

The main key for the vitality, legitimacy and safety of ongoing successes with companies and societies that economically benefit from earth and sea resource extractions, is to ensure that reasonable regulations and reclamation procedures are followed so that the economic impact is further enhanced by providing recreational and sporting opportunities. Acid rains and acid mine drainages in areas such as Pennsylvania, West Virginia and Maryland are a major concern to conservation organizations and local economies that rely on healthy, clean waterways. Many sections of the eastern United States, including the maritime provinces of Canada, have witnessed the catastrophic effects of too much acid deposited by the rain clouds originating from coal burning western states. Many streams and rivers that once held healthy populations of native fish, crustaceans, insects and all manner of ecological interactions and exchanges have become dormant and devoid of life. Fortunately, with advance technologies to make cleaner coal burning stacks possible, less acid rain is affecting what otherwise are pristine ponds, lakes and rivers of the northeast. Coal is an abundant, relatively cheap and necessary short-term component in our arsenal of choices that we must use to help with our desire to become energy independent. Continued and diligently-applied technologies that lessen pollutants must continue to be advanced to insure delivery of the cleanest burning coal possible.

The Appalachian Mountain Territory has seen its share of mineral excavation operations. Mining is important to the economic fabric of these rural hills with generations of families' livelihoods dependent upon it. Unfortunately drainages from old, closed mines have filtered into the local waterways, depleting them of life and additional local economic activity. Rivers and streams that appear vibrant and alive are dead and fallow due to human neglect and past unregulated mining practices. Mining companies today must reclaim and replenish closed sites with top soils and native vegetation in conjunction with measures to prevent any residue liquid runoff. Fortunately, reclamation success stories are now coming to the forefront. The federal Surface Mining Control and Reclamation Act (SMCRA) extracts money from active mining companies to pay the cleanup of past sins. An example of this money being wisely spent in river recovery can be found on the North Branch of the Potomac River in West Virginia and Maryland. Eight limestone dosers were placed in strategically located tributaries of the North Branch in the mid-1990s. These dosers treat the moving waters with alkaline material, raising the PH and negating the catastrophic effects of acidic metals that suffocated the river of all aquatic life. In 2009, 11,500 brown trout and 70,000 rainbows were stocked with success, and today the river is alive with fish, insects and a renewed, healthy ecosystem. The cost of keeping this major waterway active with life comes to the tune of $321,000 annually. It was tabulated that anglers and boaters now contribute $3 million a year to the economies of Garrett and Allegheny counties in western Maryland. This included $2.1 million in spending that created 40 jobs. We often hear how economic hustle and bustle with job creation is what America needs, and I agree. However, it is also an undeniable truth often overlooked and misunderstood that conservation and preservation programs properly administered add measurably to our local economies and strength as a nation and people. The ideal partnership is to have industry working alongside strong environmental initiatives that coexist to help local economies with the beautification of our landscapes, waterways and wild fish populations.

Ocean Perils

Since recorded time the oceans have been used as dumping grounds by the human race. It was once widely believed that the vastness of oceans could consume human waste and residue without damaging their life-sustaining and emergent ecosystems. Today we have come full circle with the realization that oceans and their inhabitants cannot save themselves, and that major conservation initiatives are required to lessen pollutants and toxic waste. It is estimated that 80% of marine contamination comes from land-based activity. Over fishing has taken its toll on our ocean's wide and varied species of fish and marine biodiversity. More than 75% of the world fish stocks have been exploited and many countries are now instituting quotas and timelines to reduce commercial fishing pressure on those species that have become the most jeopardized. The fisheries service branch of the National Oceanic and Atmospheric Administration (NOAA) was legally required to end overfishing of all stocks in the United States by 2014. They have reported that of the 36 species being monitored, 21 of New England's stocks now are saved from overfishing. Cod stocks have improved, but not to the degree envisioned since a 2008 population study where NOAA determined that the fish were gaining good numbers. NOAA believes that the population is now only about fifth the size it needs to rebuild, and that this requires that fisherman's catch quotas need to be reduced by 90% to reach the goal of saving fish. Commercial fisherman and a contingent of politicians are skeptical of NOAA's assessment. They have leveraged political muscle to urge the Secretary of Commerce to lessen the blow to fishing families by instituting a one year interim plan that would only cut fish catch totals between 12 and 22%. During this period NOAA will re-check all monitoring assessments to determine steps that will need to be implemented to insure that cod fish are truly on their way to recovery. There certainly is a huge disconnect between the NOAA and those whose livings are made at sea. If NOAA is right, cutting fishing quotas by only 12 to 22 percent won't cut the mustard for a species trying to recover. However, bottom dwelling fish such as Pollock, dogfish and haddock have apparently recovered in good numbers and they inhabit many of the same waters as cod. When the fishing nets drag the bottoms, all fish are claimed and monitored. Logic would seem to point to cod recuperating in conjunction with these other species, but nature sometimes confers different numbers than we expect. Only time will tell. From this writer's perspective it would appear that a safer 40 – 50% reduction would be appropriate given all factors in this argument, since all parties agree that cod have just begun to recover over the past few years. If NOAA is right about the 90% cut, commercial fisherman will be only jeopardizing their life lines further. It is in everyone's interest to once again have healthy cod stocks and to implement long-term conservation measures to insure that these most delicious and historic bastions of the deep sea stay with us for eternity.

Globally, a network of 'marine parks' or reserves covering the most critical ocean sectors would help measurably with restoring life biodiversity. Closed reserves and parks have already proven great recovery tools in various parts of the globe such as those in the Red Sea, the Caribbean, Australia and on the west coast in California.

Forage Fish

In the world of recreational fishing in coastal New England, we are beginning to witness the hopeful recovery of haddock and cod stocks. Since the George's Bank disaster and subsequent moratorium on fishing and dragging imposed the mid 1990s, these fish and other bottom dwellers have had the chance to regain some of their former glory. However, the Grand Banks of Newfoundland were so damaged that even after two decades of near-closure to fishing, these once hallowed grounds for Cod and Haddock have not yet recovered. Through the late 1980s and 1990s there were healthy populations of stripped bass, mackerel, blue fish, pollock and tuna. In the last few years there has been a drastic drop in the numbers of stripers and tuna, which is related to too much commercial boat activity and diseased striper stock resulting from pollutants in Maryland's Chesapeake Bay area. According to the National Oceanic and Atmospheric Administration (NOAA) the striped bass recreational catch has declined by 70% since 2006 which is, in part, related to several years of poor spawning success. But, it is also likely that game fish and other ocean predators have become threatened by depleting numbers of forage fish. The main source of food for most all predator fish from Canada to Florida are menhaden (pogies) and Atlantic herring. Currently these staples of the food chain are being netted commercially in the millions of pounds annually to fill the demands for fishmeal, fertilizer, pet and farm animal feed, dietary supplement additives and lobster bait. The Atlantic States Marine Fisheries Commission (ASMFC) concurs that overfishing of menhaden is occurring and they are working out new measures of harvest reduction. Their continued depletion would have catastrophic affects on game fish populations, recreational angling and commercial netting. Local economies stand to lose millions. When menhaden were plentiful their surface wake schools could cover ¼ to ½ square miles. Now we are lucky to see 20 to 40 yards of activity. Strong conservation measures need to be implemented quickly to save what many believe to be the key link to healthy stocks of game fish along the Atlantic seaboard. Since each state regulates their own fisheries programs, elected officials from these states along the coast need to be contacted by all concerned sportsman to alert them to the realities of diminishing fish and the drastic economic consequences of indecisiveness and inaction.

Atlantic Salmon

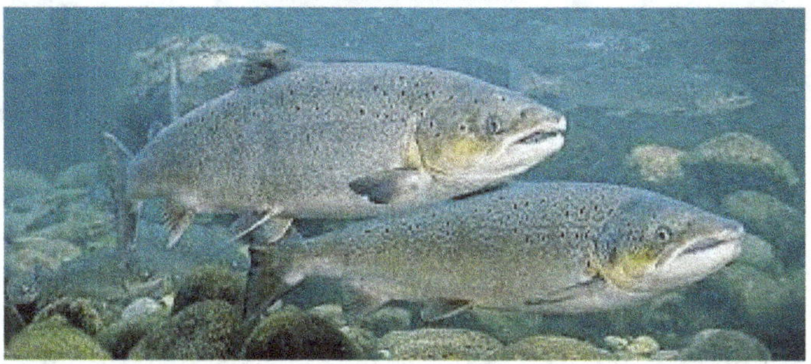

Eastern Canada's livelihood flows and eddies with the number of Atlantic salmon that inhabit its many pristine rivers and tributaries. Over $125 million is spent here annually by recreational anglers in pursuit of this iconic species. The total net worth amounts to over $250 million with over 3800 full-time jobs related to healthy fish numbers and clean, vibrant rivers. Commercial sea and river netting of these fish has been reduced dramatically over that past decade because of wisely instituted programs that buy out individual netters and fleets, coupled with many countries placing moratoriums on netting wild salmon. As is again often the case when it involves our natural resources and the bounties of wild animals and fish, drastic regulatory procedures have been needed to save species from excess exploitation and extinction. It is important to point out that historically, governments were not concerned with conservation efforts on behalf of wild salmon. It was only when the public became aware of the problem of diminishing salmon numbers by organizations such as the North Atlantic Salmon Fund (NASF) and the Atlantic Salmon Federation (ASF) did governments begin to take notice and begin an active role in financing and recovery efforts. In this process of saving wild Atlantic salmon, many governments have learned that healthy numbers of returning river fish greatly enhance the economies of local towns. With that said, many people benefit from the dollars gained from sportsmen who travel worldwide in pursuit of this majestic silver swimmer. It is wise and necessary to always include government officials in mitigating and recovery procedures, since political muscle properly directed proves to be of great benefit to game species and ultimately to all of mankind.

Spotted Owls

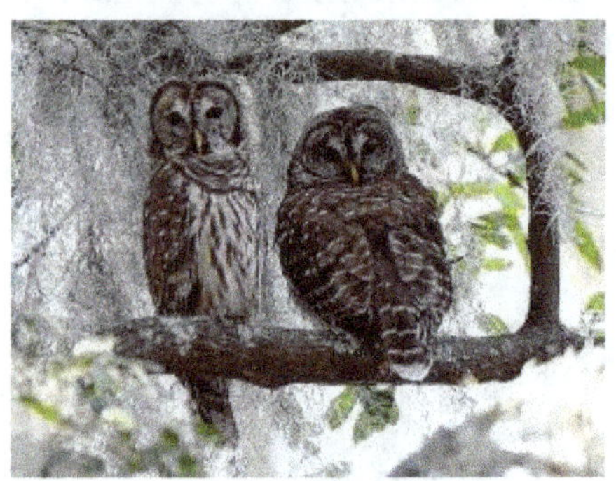

Barred Owls
Pages.vassar.edu

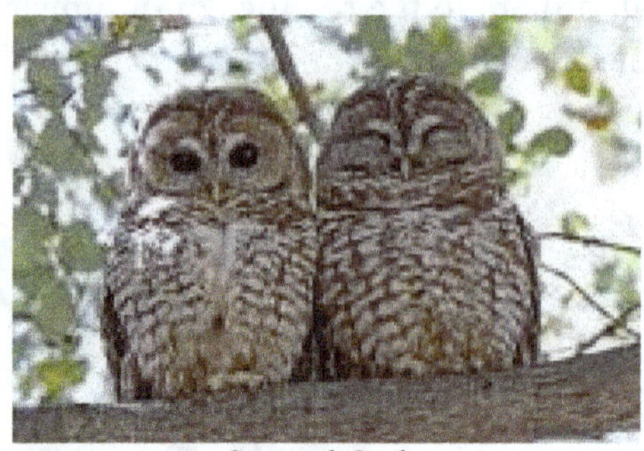

Spotted Owls
speezees.com

There is something positive to be said about the 'wise use of our natural resources.' I learned at an early age that most forests require management in order to remain healthy and vital. Federal and state-regulated forestry procedures are implemented in each state to insure that logging and production mills meet standards that safeguard the resource, while at the same time allowing free enterprise the opportunity to provide needed lumber supplies to a growing population. Trees are a renewable resource, and with proper forestry practices implemented, they grow back again, providing food and shelter for all wildlife, including owls. Twenty years ago environmentalists teamed up with the federal government and the Endangered Species Act to supposedly save Oregon and Washington's Spotted Owls from extinction. To insure the owls recovery, close to 6 million acres of land was closed to logging. Of the 200 or so sawmills that were in operation in Oregon, less than 80 are in business today. Needless to say, thousands of good-paying jobs were eliminated in rural areas that relied on the timber industry for sustenance, resulting in a rising unemployment of over 20% in many counties. Do you think that politics would have ever allowed the closing of 90% of the mining facilities in rural West Virginia, Pennsylvania and Ohio if the Spotted Owl was threatened there? Not a chance. The representatives, senators and working people in these states would never have allowed their economy and neighbors to suffer because of the alleged plight of a single bird.

So what is the status of the Spotted Owl today? We must be looking at a success story. Nope, their population continues to decline. How can this be? In these northwestern forests, the owls are disappearing on the average rate of 3% a year. No one has answers as to why. In the meantime, forest fires have destroyed over 70 pairs of these owls, with the largest blaze scarring over 500,000 acres in 2002. This fire alone cost $150 million to fight and destroyed over 4 billion dollars worth of timber. When a forest is left unmanaged, trees mature, begin to decline and eventually succumb to the ravages of old age. When they tumble and fall, one over the other, they soon lose their moisture and become ever-increasingly brittle and useless as lumber. As such, these forests immerge into mammoth fire traps that are virtually impossible to control once lighting strikes or a misplaced cinder finds its place in the underbrush. So with all this evidence in hand after a 20 year failure to resurrect the spotted owl, what do you suppose the U.S. Fish and Wildlife Service has issued in its final plan to save the owl? The Revised Recovery Plan of June 30, 2011 increases the owls protective acreage over the approximately 6 million acres currently in place. It calls for eradication via shooting hundreds of barred owls that are doing well in this habitat and who are rivals of the spotted owls for nesting sites and food. The Fish and Wildlife Service believes with no guarantees that the spotted owl populations could be revitalized at a cost of $127 million over the next 30 years. If the stimulus package instituted 22 years ago didn't work, why would another similarly long winded, nonsensical expanded copy work for another 30 years? Where is the Audubon Society to protest the shooting of their beloved barred owls? Where are the tried and true environmentalists who care so much for our natural world and all its inhabitants? Where is Congress to right these wrongs and reverse this madness and wasted taxpayer dollars?

Is this drama really about saving the spotted owl or is the poor owl being used as a prop in a wilderness theater production designed to simply preserve the forests from human encroachment and lumber management? If so, who and what benefit? It is clear that no entity benefits, and this whole process is irrational and beyond the scope of any comprehension or understanding. If this show was on Broadway, how long do you think it would have taken to close the doors when nobody showed up? The Spotted Owl may indeed be endangered, but the evidence suggests that nature would rather handle the evolution process rather than having any human interference. The northwest economy and its families have lost billions of lumber dollars, unemployment is rapid and our tax dollars are continuing to pay for the foibles of unbridled federal government mismanagement and deception. The Fish & Wildlife Service's resources could be used in much more productive and beneficial ways. There is a place for the Endangered Species Act, but here it was misused, misplaced and rightly made a joke of. Does anyone question that we need to fast track an 'Endangered Logic Act' or 'Endangered Common Sense Act' to place on the other side of the pendulum to give these faulty, costly decisions some counter balance? This whole scheme to preserve the forests has backfired. The sad truth is that this federal program enacted 24 years ago, and which is being blindly peddled again, is essentially anything but preservation. To 'preserve' forests and its intertwined ecologies, conservation initiatives must be implemented to protect and grow trees, while at the same time harvesting wood from various sections of the forest grid. This doesn't necessarily mean that every forest segment is or should be harvestable. Land can be set aside and designated as 'parklands', where commercial cutting and clearing is not allowed and where recreation is encouraged. Furthermore, 'forest reserves' have their place of importance, whereby timber harvesting is excluded and natural processes take precedence. We see the evidence of this 'natural setting' in such places as the Redwood and Sequoia forests of northern California where many of these majestic and largest of trees are over 3000 years old. Although parklands and forest reserves are chosen as commercial-free zones, these land masses still require periodic chain saw work to remove felled trees and blow-down sectors. These measures are necessary to help prevent fires and to make the land safe and accessible for hikers and other interlopers.

> *Preservation is not always conservation,*
> *but conservation is always preservation…*

> ~Tom Johnson

Chapter 2

Deer Runs - River Runs

My first glance of the spectacular Gaspe Peninsula, Quebec came in October, 2001 when friends and I decided to archery hunt for deer on nearby Anticosti Island. The first recall and interest pertaining to this island were lucid memories of my dad's successful rifle hunting trip here 50 years ago.

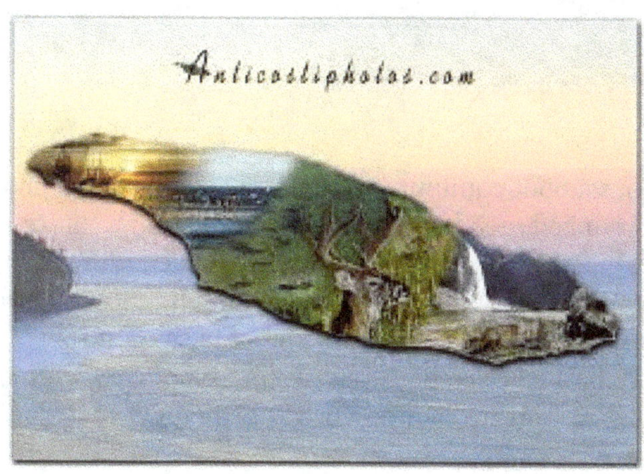

We booked our trip with Sepaq Anticosti Outfitters and stayed at their La Loutre River Lodge. The 3000-square-mile, elongated island just north of the Gaspe with its 320 miles of shoreline sits dominantly in the Gulf of the St. Lawrence River waterway. The island has a storied history of its indigenous peoples, explorers, various ownerships with forestry and fisheries interests predominating the economy. In 1895 Frenchman Henri Menier purchased the island and introduced 220 white-tailed deer. One of the earth's most adaptable animals, the deer flourished. Today's population exceeds 160,000 with about 11,000 harvested annually by hunters. Of all the native and introduced wildlife, none did as well to dominate the landscape as did America's greatest big game animal. The deer have no natural predators here, so it is important to try to keep the herd in healthy numbers by culling them through hunting. The only other wildlife we saw in numbers was the native red fox. Unlike many of their New England cousins, these fox appeared more robust and healthy, with prominent, beautiful and thick red-gray hair and long, fluffy tails. Their striking appearance may be due to the great ocean food resources rendering the best in nutrition. We did notice that the venison we harvested had a remarkably succulent, tender taste. The tasty tender meat must be attributed to the abundant beach-front food and nutrients they consume.

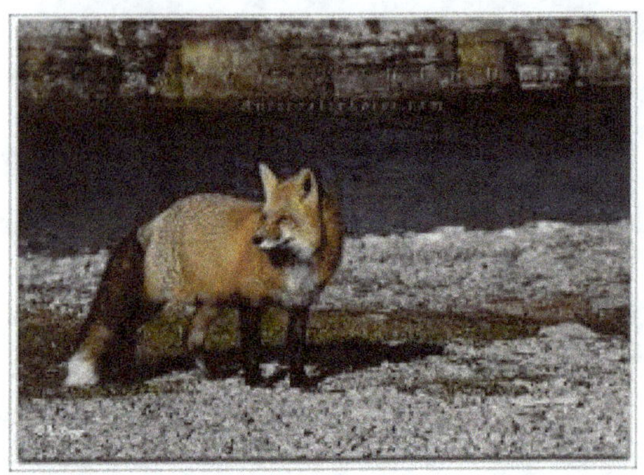
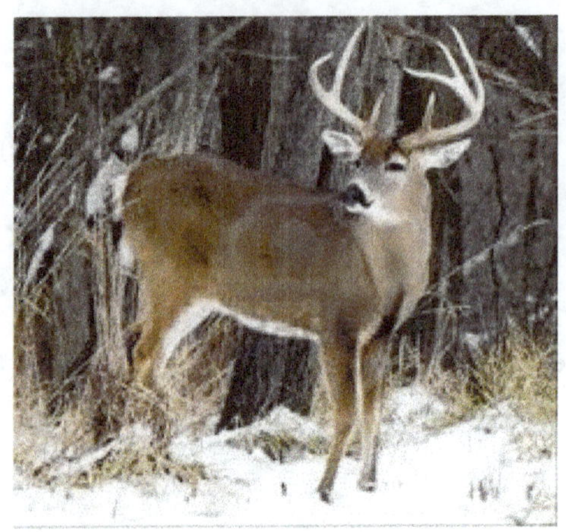

I was thinking about combining the hunt with Atlantic salmon and trout fishing. My buddies convinced me to forgo the fishing for some future trip. I was itching to throw a fly into the flowing La Loutre waters. Instead I hunted at a slow pace along its banks keeping a watchful eye for any movement, including trout dashing away from my shadows. This island has some notable salmon runs when the weather cooperates. The best river is the Jupiter where there can be great fishing if it rains enough to bring the river levels up—the rivers being largely 'spate' in nature.

The hunting we experienced was almost fantasy. We had at our disposal over 100 square miles of boreal forest designated as archery only hunting. The forests were so thick with white and black spruce and balsam fir that the outfitter had to bulldoze paths through the woods in order for us to penetrate them. There were, however, a plentiful number of openings in the landscape along the way to spot and get an arrow off in the direction of a standing deer. I have been an archer in pursuit of whitetails for over 40 years and this was my only successful experience in stalking on foot this cagey animal. Deer runs and tracks were everywhere, and we were excited to be in this hunting paradise.

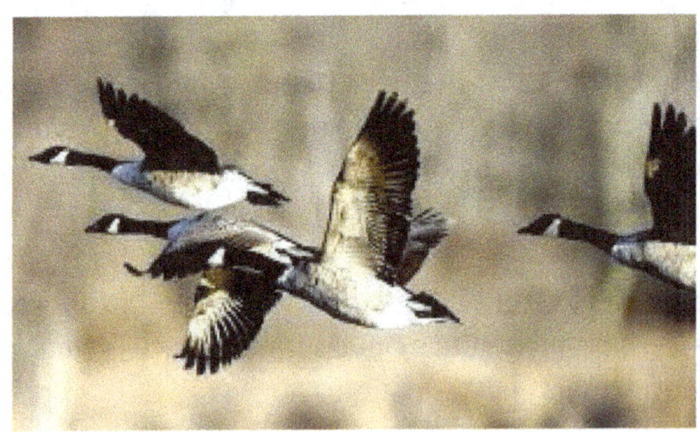

My first success was in the deep woods off a logging road where I pussyfooted along for over an hour before eyeing a 6-point buck facing away broadside at 25 yards. The moist, green-mossy ground made for quiet stepping, and the deer was unaware of my presence. Moseying along for several hundred yards prior to this encounter, a number of deer ran across in front of me. One nicely-racked buck was off in the distance rubbing his antlers and scent on some high evergreen branches. I knelt down and crawled to what cover was available and began rattling with a pair of antlers that I always carry. The buck came up on a knoll 15 yards away, spotted me and was off across the tote road in a flash. If I was able to secure better cover, I may have been able to connect with an arrow. I was disappointed but also elated by this adrenalin rush. This is what hunting is all about—the pursuit and the challenge is often what's most rewarding. A short time later as I was quietly shuffling along the edge of a thicket, the opportunity with another broadsided standing buck was picture book perfect. With one arrow released, the animal leaped and dropped after a short dash within eyesight.

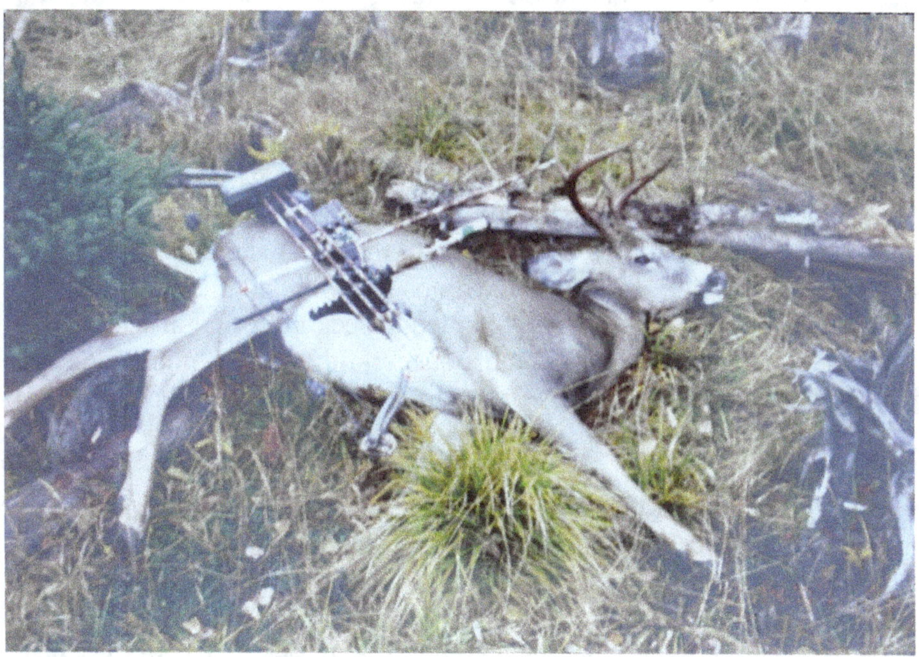

The second success was a couple days later as I was overlooking the ocean beach closer to the lodge. A buck was eating his way along the water's edge 40 yards away. The wind coming due south off the St. Lawrence Gulf was beating strongly against my face as the sweet smell of the sea penetrated my nostrils. Using the wind and its noise to my advantage, I was able to sneak within 20 yards of the deer. When the animal fed on seaweed, I crawled closer. When he looked up and about, I stopped still behind small clumps of sea grass. As the red sun was beginning to set with its strong reflection radiating off the water's edge, I waited for what I hoped would be the perfect moment, came to a kneeled position and drew the bow string back. At that instant the wind gusts became even stronger, blowing my hat off and whipping the bow back and forth. I relaxed the string, bent low, wiped my eyes, and tried to regain some composure as my heart began to race. "Ok Tom, nice and easy now," I said to myself. I sucked in a deep breath of air, kneeled up again, drew the bow back, slowly exhaled and let the arrow fly. The deer whirled around, did a semi-circle up behind me and dropped at 35 yards. It happened so fast, and the drama of the moment lingered with me in the dusk. The arrow found its final home some distance out in the St. Lawrence River. As I let the arrow go it was pointing at the Gaspe Peninsula—a distant shoreline across the Gulf that we would be visiting soon.

My brother-in-law Doug and friends Glenn and Ray also had plenty of exciting hunting, but the deer were not always cooperating with their plans. With persistence in varying their landscape and technique from day to day, they eventually had their share of venison to transport back to the States. Deer are simply an amazing and cagey animal with keen memories. I was reminded of their craftiness more than halfway through the week. Doug had not yet connected with an opportunity, and he was itching to get off a clean shot. Even though the areas we hunted were heavily infested with deer, the deer avoided many of the tree stands that the guides had guided us into. After a few days we all came to the conclusion that deer had been disturbed one too many times at these locations and were not likely to show themselves. From that realization we all opted to seek more virgin sections of woods and with these moves, we all became more successful. One evening Doug was sitting in one of these 'guided stands' for several hours. He decided before darkness set in to climb down the tree and creep up a major run a short distance away. Within ten minutes he heard a branch crack straight ahead uphill through some deadfalls. He stopped, slumped down low on his knees and saw the outline of a beautiful 8 point buck standing broadside at 35 yards. Coming to a semi-standing position he pulled back the bow and let the arrow fly. The buck dropped in his tracks—a perfectly placed kill shot. Doug was elated and definitely relieved. He made the right move in vacating a stand that the deer had become wary of. Success was his.

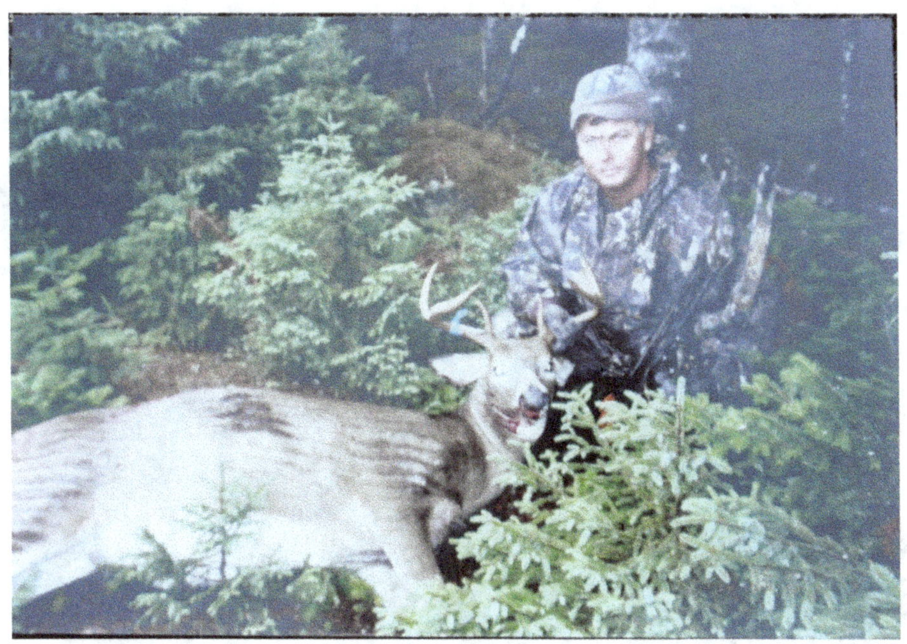

In camp with us were two guys from Alabama who told hilarious (albeit dangerous) stories about hunting the swamps of the deep south for deer, boar and rattlesnakes. With our eyes intently upon them and snickers on our faces, they would demonstrate with their arms, hands, and feet—describing in every detail in their deep southern drawl the many encounters and close calls they had with wild boar that chased them to and from their tree stands. They hunted rattlesnakes and sold them on the open market, often leaving them alive and coiled up in the backseats of their pickup truck. "We'd calect all these rattlas and sometimes leave em awile sleepin on the back seat so our guns wouldn't be stolen whiles we was enjoyen some beers in town after a day's huntin." These guys were true down home redneck entertainment at its finest. The more we laughed, the more they laughed, and then the French couple from the Montreal area would chime in with a few chosen stories about their adventurous day of hunting on the island, and the laughter would grow louder. Here we were with three noticeably clear-speaking accents representing the South, Quebec and New England, and as we talked and told stories our smiles were ignited, not just by the adventurous and often funny hunting episodes shared, but by the deeply rooted dialects that made for humorous discourse. This camaraderie that grew with each day was an added bonus.

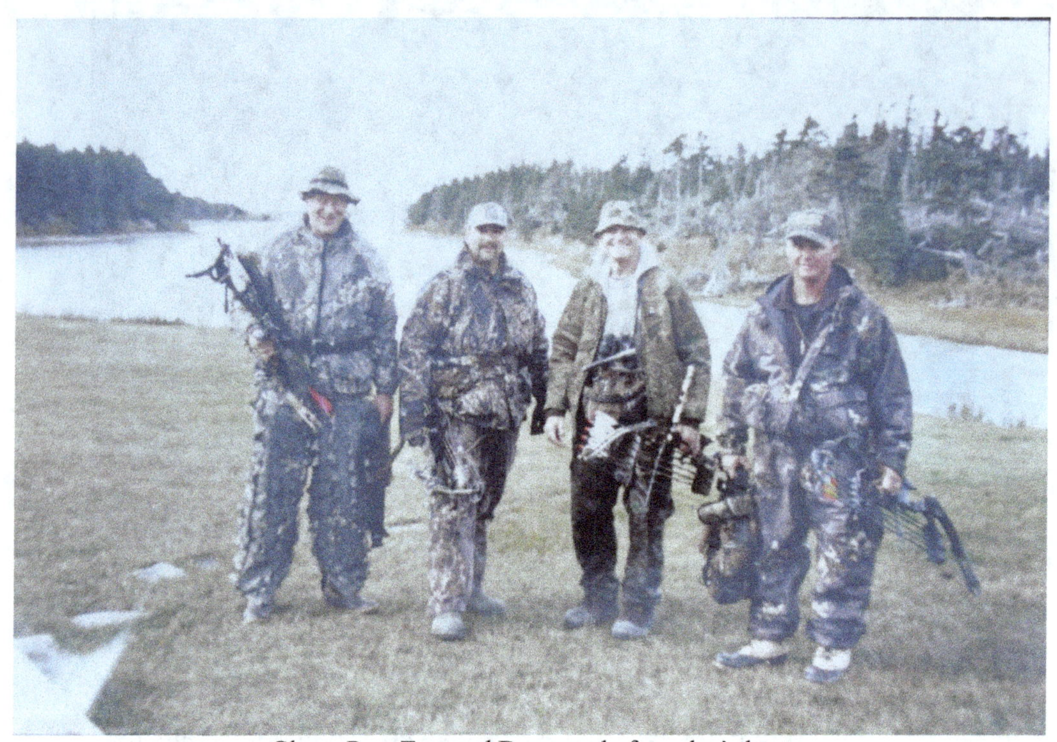

Glenn, Ray, Tom and Doug ready for a day's hunt

Gaspe Magnific

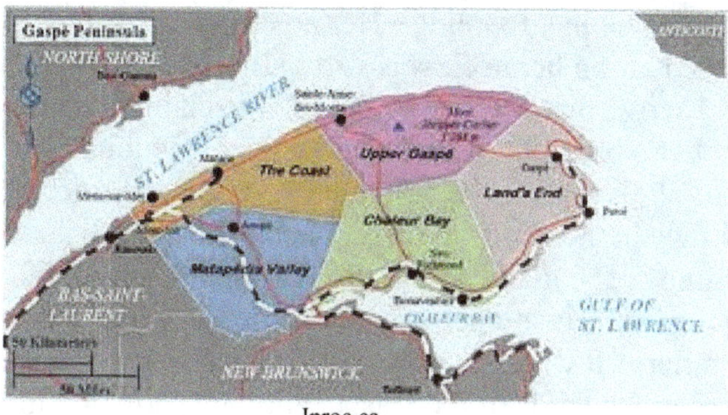

Jproc.ca

The week flew by as weeks usually do when your engaged with your friends in
doing what you love in the great out-of-doors. The guides did a great job providing
for us and preparing the steaks and chops for the flight back home. We had one day
to relax before the flight to Montreal and Boston, so we elected to rent a car and
travel the northern coast of the Gaspe Peninsula. We had studied some of the terrain
and rivers here and wanted to learn something more about the storied salmon runs
and how they were monitored and conserved. Native Indians named this land Gaspe
which means 'lands end,' indicating where the mountains are engulfed by the sea at
Quebec's most easterly point. We visited the Matane, Cap-Chat and Sainte-Anne
river valleys, campgrounds and cabin facilities in anticipation of fishing here in the
near future. Most rivers are operated by non-profit management groups called ZECs
(acronym for the French zone d'exploitation controlee). They divide their rivers into
sectors or zones and it's determined by how many fisherman will be allowed in any
given river section. Public access is gained via a daily fee which varies from river to
river or through a November lottery. What was the most striking to us was the
clarity of the gin-clear waters cascading down into and around classic dry-fly casting
valleys. Climbing up and through the picturesque Chic-Choc park mountain range
we followed the Sainte-Anne River for several miles. The Parc de la Gaspesie is
a prime piece of conservation land. Its picturesque Appalachian mountain range is
the highest in Quebec and several salmon rivers originate from this hilly
country. The park is home to the last Caribou living south of the St. Lawrence River
and is populated by many moose. Along the way through the park Ray spotted a
moose just inside the wood line. Not believing him we reluctantly backed up the car,
and sure enough, there was mother moose. "I told you so!" exclaimed Ray.

"Ray, you have hawk eyes!" I exclaimed. It's no big deal to see a moose in this
terrain, but a couple of the guys including Ray had never seen one in the wild, so for

them this was a novel interlude. We all got out to take pictures and Doug and I soon got caught between the moose and her calf. She ran right at us as we spun around and ducked quickly behind a sapling. Her nostrils were spuming mist in our direction, and the hair on her neck was vertically rigid with madness, just a few feet from our eyes. "Wow, that was close, Doug," I exclaimed. "I didn't see the calf until it was too late. Let's back out of here and leave them alone."

"Ya, let's go. She's scaring the crap out of me," Doug uttered. As the moose retreated, so did we in the opposite direction. It was moose hunting season on the Gaspe, but hunting was not allowed in this Chic-Choc preserve. As we ventured out on to the main road we saw numerous cars and trucks with moose racks sticking up on hoods and trailers. It was apparent that moose hunting was a ritual and serious undertaking here in the wilds of the Gaspe, and that showing them off was the norm and not the exception. Stopping at Tim Hortons for a coffee and snack before boarding the plane, I was secretly making plans to come back to hunt these moose and fish these rivers as soon as time would allow.

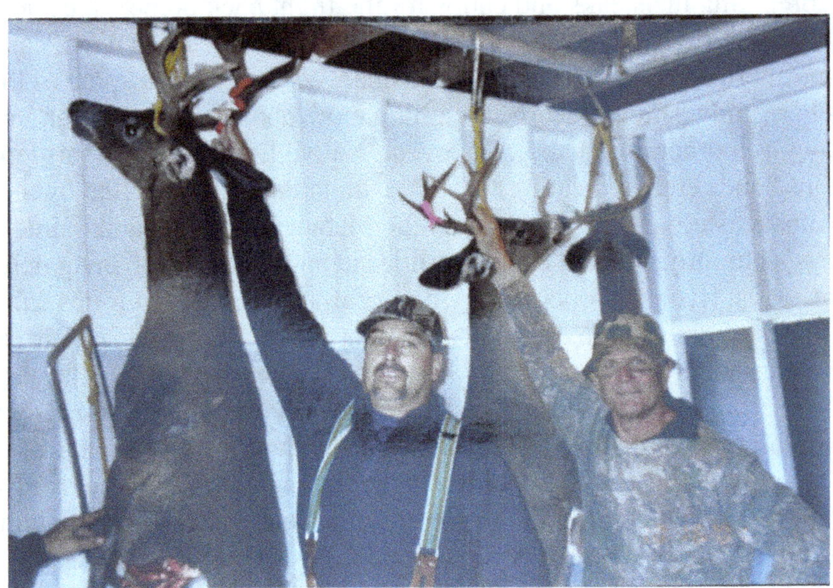

Ray & Tom with their deer

Petite-Cascapedia

Although the Gaspe beckoned, my friends had other fishing destinations planned for me. So it took a few years to sort out a time to get back here. Our Sutton friends John and acclaimed artist Linda Sinacola stayed with my wife and I at our Maine retreat for several days before John and I ventured off for our first Gaspe fishing adventure.

I had entered the November fishing draw, but my number drawn was too high on the list to secure any 'prime water' dates. We choose the end of June into early July to just 'wing it' and see what rivers we could get on from day to day along the southern coast. The only early reservations we made were with a couple of hotels, and the services of legendary guide Steeve Bujold on the East branch of the Petite Cascapedia River. We also stayed riverside at Zec Petite Cascapedia's Camp Melancon which proved to be the perfect spot to enjoy the mixed ambiance of the history, sights and sounds of this famous salmon river. We hoped that we would be able to catch not only salmon but also some of the large sea-run brook trout that prefer this river over many of the other rivers on the peninsula.

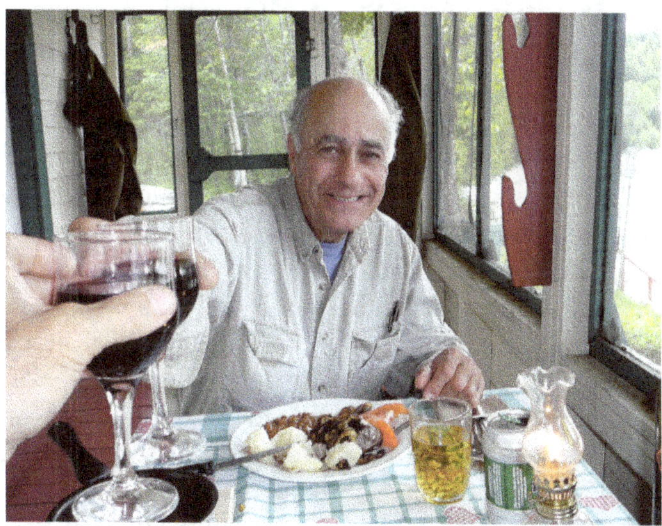
John and I saluting at our first evening at Camp Melancon

The Gaspe has a large selection of crystal clear salmon rivers that are in close proximity to each other stretching north, west and south along the semi-circle circumference of this peninsula. Along the northern shore from west to east are the rivers Matane, Cap-Chat, Saint-Anne, and Madeleine. The terrain here is more rugged and dramatic than the more tranquil, pastoral southern coastline. On the western shore we proceeded to the town of Gaspe where the Dartmouth, York and Saint-Jean rivers run into the Atlantic Ocean. Along the southern shoreline proceeding west to east we crossed the rivers Grande, Pabos, Bonaventure, Petite-Cascapedia, Grande-Cascapedia, Novelle, Matapedia and Patapedia.   Small villages that hug the coast show their dominance with at least one church steeple reaching toward the skies, thus symbolizing the people's faith in a God that brought all these scenic vistas to their doorsteps. With so many inviting rivers to choose from, it can be difficult making the choice on which rivers to fish. Since these waters typically fish best at different weeks with much depending upon weather conditions, it is best to call ahead before booking a time on any particular river or section of the peninsula. Knowing in advance what to expect will help narrow down the best options.

John and I were hoping to catch the early season big run of sea-run brook trout with a mix of fresh salmon on the Petite-Cascapedia. We met our guide, Steeve Bujold, and his dog, Partner, at the Zec headquarters. We motored many miles upstream before finding a suitable place to launch Steeve's classic square-back canoe for a two-day adventure. Partner jumped off the truck several miles before the launching site and hunted along the way, flushing up spruce partridge and chasing hare until he caught up to us while we were readying the canoe to go. He jumped in and took his practiced position next to Steeve. It was mid-morning as our guide polled us out onto the river. John and I were amazed at how beautiful and pristine the river was — emerald green, gin clear waters with fast cascading falls mellowing out into deep, wide pools just waiting for our flies to skip across. The weather was clear and crisp — just perfect for such an excursion as this. We readied our fly rods as Steeve stood in the back, polling the canoe from one side of the river to the other, peering into the depths looking for outlines of sea-trout and salmon. At likely fish-holding spots he would let the back anchor down to hold us steady against the current as John and I casted into the eddies, pools and bankings. After repeating these maneuvers for a couple miles with only a couple native trout caught and released, I was beginning to wonder where the big fish were. Steeve had spotted a few sea-run trout but had spooked them getting too close with the canoe. "Nothing in numbers yet," said Steeve. "This time of year things can change very fast though, and we can run into hundreds of fish." With noon approaching, we pulled the canoe up on a rocky beach for a lunch break as our trusty guide quickly prepared a tee-pee fire with hot tea, sandwiches and cookies to satisfy our hunger.

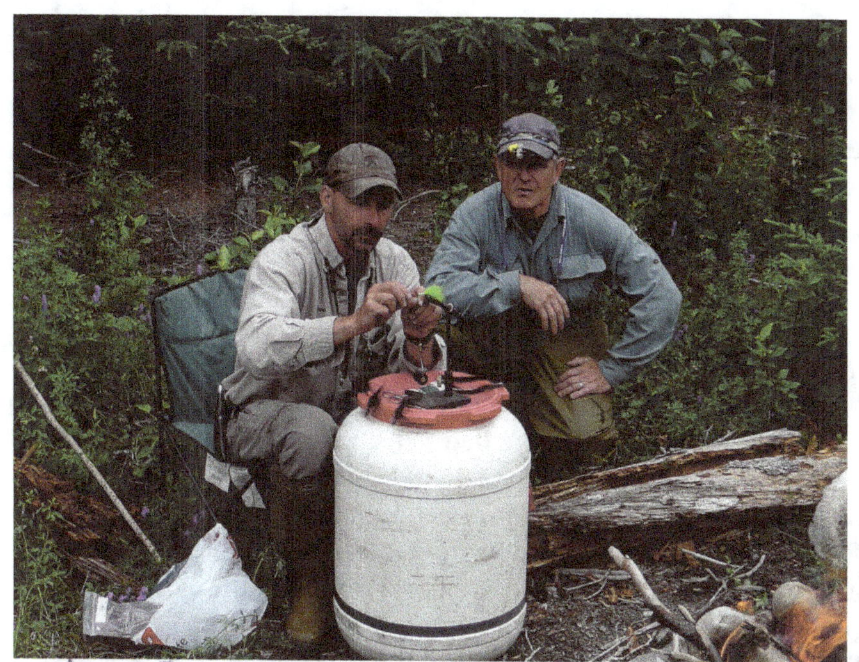

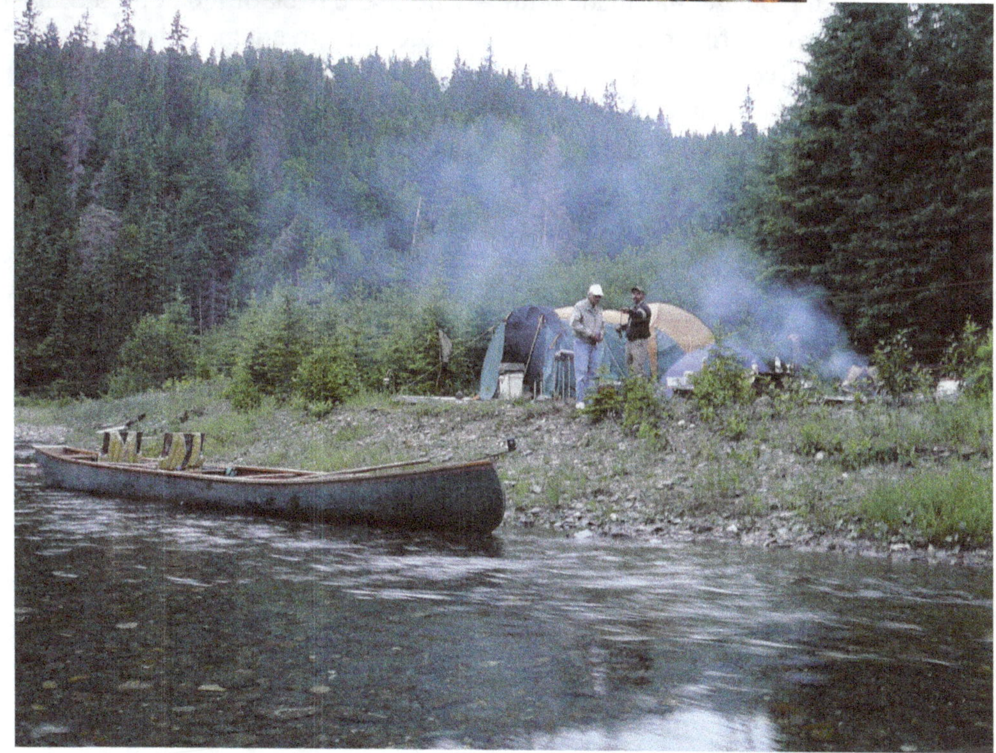

Camp set for dinner, fly tying and rest

For the remainder of the afternoon we meandered downstream past steep, majestic mountains, taking in all the glory of this special place as we cast a variety of streamers and wooly buggers to likely fish-holding spots. We hooked and netted some nice trout but no salmon. It appeared, and was later confirmed, that very few salmon had yet ascended the river from the ocean bay. Although the fishing was slow, the scenery, adventure and positive anticipation for what tomorrow might bring kept our spirits high. We set up camp for the evening at about the halfway point and started a 'driftwood fire'. I had brought along venison steaks from last fall's success in the Maine woods, and along with Steeve's garden vegetables, we feasted like kings as the sun began to close its eyes. Partner was just a delightful dog and made a great companion for all of us. John especially took a liking to him, patting her ears and neck as she finally began to slow down and lie between John and the fire, sensing it was time to get ready for a night's rest. Steeve set up his make-shift tying fly vise and quickly fashioned some large, green-tinseled wooly buggers just as the moon began to show. "If I had just one fly to fish with, this would be the one," Steeve stated. "When you cast these out diagonally across a pool, just let the current take the fly down and pump your arm back and forth with pulsating action. No need to strip line in until the bugger has made a full swing to the back of the pool. I'll make up a few for tomorrow's fishing." John and I nodded in agreement. These 'buggers' are extremely effective with all kinds of fish. I would have preferred, however, to have had the chance to hook into a large salmon using a dry fly like a bomber or wulff pattern. There is still nothing quite like having a game fish slam a fly on the surface. For my money it provides the best adrenalin rush in fishing and always keeps you focused and on your toes. As darkness finally came with moonbeams dimpling on the river below us, we fell asleep listening to the sound of a river that has been alive with motion and life since the last ice age.

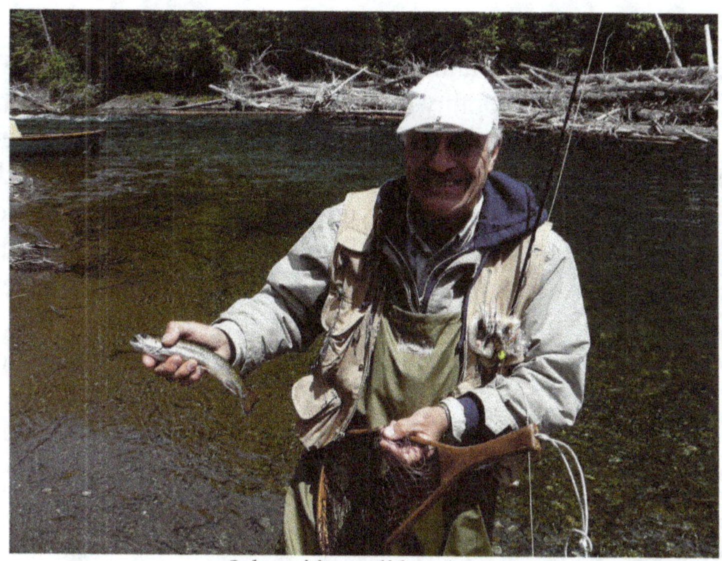

John with small brook trout

Dawn broke with a cool temperature in the low 50s and with clouds of mist hiding much of the river from our view. After a hardy breakfast and coffee to help get our bodies moving, we again cast our lot upon the river, canoeing and wading several more miles before coming to the covered bridge at Zec headquarters. The fishing stayed slow with the occasional sea-run trout hooked and released and no salmon. We were all disappointed that the salmon hadn't yet ascended the river. We learned later that the runs were uncharacteristically late that year and that it took several more weeks for salmon to show up in numbers. This was true on most of the Gaspe rivers in 2007. Thanking Steeve for his great navigation and fun and after hugging Partner goodbye, John and I reluctantly headed back to the States.

"I have fished through fishless days that I remember happily without regret."

~Roger Haig-Brown

John's Memory

John had been fishing with me for several years as he was approaching retirement age. I first met him and his wife Linda in the 1980s at our local Sutton Water's Farm event. For years we were involved with preservation efforts at this 1750 farm and farmhouse and Linda would often display her magnificent painting scenes depicting historic New England landscapes and buildings at fundraising events there. John was a 'jack of all trades' and a 'johnny on the spot'. Over the course of his life he gladly helped his town, family and friends with various building and electrical projects. He often didn't take enough time for himself, and Linda would encourage him to go fishing with me. So for several years John joined me as we ventured to Maine, Alaska and Canada to seek the best locations holding native trout and salmon. Within two years of our Gaspe trip, John was diagnosed with stomach cancer that got progressively worse as time went on. After several operations and a gallant battle against the ravages of his body, John died peacefully at home with his loving wife Linda at his side. A man of deep faith and devotion, he had told me: "Tom, it is what is is. The good Lord will take care of me, but I worry about Linda. I want her to keep busy painting and doing what she loves to do. I'll certainly miss fishing with you and the guys, but I'm sure the fishing is great where I'm going. Thanks for being my friend." John confirmed these deep feelings and more with seemingly little remorse in his last conversations with his beloved wife, Linda.

Good fishing companions and great friends are not easy to come by. Most people can count the number of close friends on the end of their fingernail. Yes, John was an ardent, proficient fisherman and outdoorsman, but he was much more important than that. He embodied all that life is and what it is supposed to mean. He gave his all and shared his all and did it with a smile. To fish with a man of such character, faith, knowledge and good humor was a blessing to all of us, and we will always deeply miss him. I often think of John now when casting my fly across waters. Sometimes this saddens me as I reminisce in a melancholy moment, but more often it brings a smile to my face. His courage and acts of giving taught me much and for that I am grateful. Sadness and disappointments are expected to intercede with in our lives, but we are never fully prepared to deal with them. I can hear John telling me again: "Hey, I'm doing fine, just fine. Relish your zest for adventure and the things in life that make it truly worth living, for we never know when it will end. Thanks for all those special times we shared."

"A real friend is one who walks in when the rest of the world walks out."

~ Walter Winchel

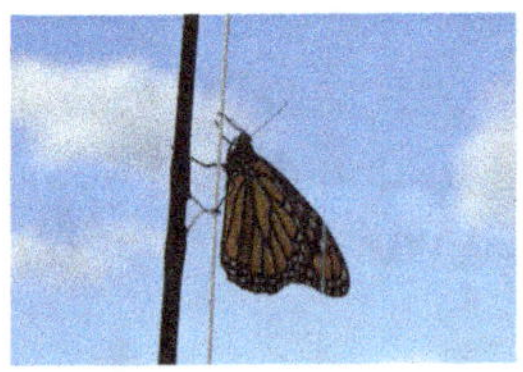

Chapter 4

Montana Sky

I'd been thinking about fishing out west for some time. Having only cast a fly in this massively large, wide and open territory one time a few years ago, there was a need to spend some quality days exploring some of its great rivers and small creeks. There was also the desire to see and experience the expanse and magnificent vistas of Montana, Idaho and Wyoming during the cooler September weather. Realizing how busy the national parks can get during the prime summer months also prompted my wife Pam and I to venture there when the traffic had significantly subsided. We thought that it would be a great idea to recruit our friends and fellow fly-fishers Ned and Elizabeth Bacon to join us on our adventure. No sooner had they said, "Yes, we would love to go with you guys," did Ned take over the chore of arranging the route we would take and the rustic retreats we would stay at. Ned grew up in the Chicago area and his dad would often take his sons fly fishing to Montana. Not only did Ned know the territory, but his family had roots there that went back to the turn of the last century. His grandfather once had a farm in the Bitterroot Valley, and it's a place where his family still owns land. Based on his background, I knew we would be in good hands with Ned's travel and fishing arrangements.

My wife Pam was getting a bit more serious about fly fishing and much of her gear needed some updating—those old leaky boots just wouldn't make the grade for this trip. Our friend Jim Bender at The Lower Forty outfitter shop in Worcester, MA set her up from top to bottom with functional gear, and she had one of my 5 weight fast-action rods to complement everything else. After several weeks of planning, we were ready to go.

Our basic plan was to fly into Missoula, rent an SUV and take Route 93 south through the Bitterroot Valley. From there, we'd zigzag our way through the southwest part of Montana before trekking through Yellowstone Park and onward to Jackson Hole, Wyoming. All told, we were looking at about 500 miles of travel, based on the principal that we wanted to fish many rivers but also experience as much of the West as we could in the 15 days allotted to us. In order to do this we would stay 2 to 3 days at one location before moving on. Even in hindsight, this itinerary turned out to be a good idea for first time sojourners looking to experience as much as possible. However, for those wanting to fish more than travel, I recommend picking a central area with fishing and other sporting locations spanning out like the spooks of a wagon wheel. In this vast western expanse there are many of these locations to choose from.

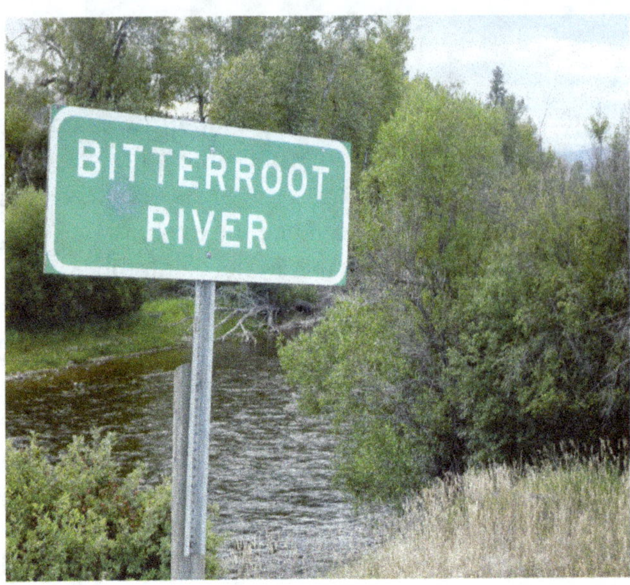

Heading south from Missoula, we followed the Bitterroot River to the town of Hamilton where we picked up licenses, food for the cabin, and flies for the river. The further south we travelled, the wilder the countryside became, until at last we found our cabin at Rocky Knob near Sula. Our hosts Margie and John Mikesell have several comfortable log cabins across the road from the river. What stands out immediately from the novel eyes of an easterner are the expansive, wide open sagebrush meadows, rugged and rocky distant mountains and tall Ponderosa pine trees interlaced with burned-out trees —the remains of wide-sweeping fires that ravaged this valley a decade or two ago. Periodic forest fires are often natural occurrences, and I learned that fires are needed in order for the Ponderosa cone droppings to open and germinate. The panoramic views are enhanced and heightened by the ever-changing daylight colors and shadows, as morning's cool weather and misty fog disappear with a strengthening mid-morning sun. There were several days when we welcomed the warmth of the sun, as we prodded our way wading in these cold mountain waters. The Bitterroot River is a mid-size, pebble-strewn stream with many slotted and elongated pools that taper their way often into larger swirling undercurrents. Each of the rivers we fished had their own distinct personalities and this one suited me to a T since I prefer medium-sized waters where I can cover all of the likely trout-holding seams from one wading location.

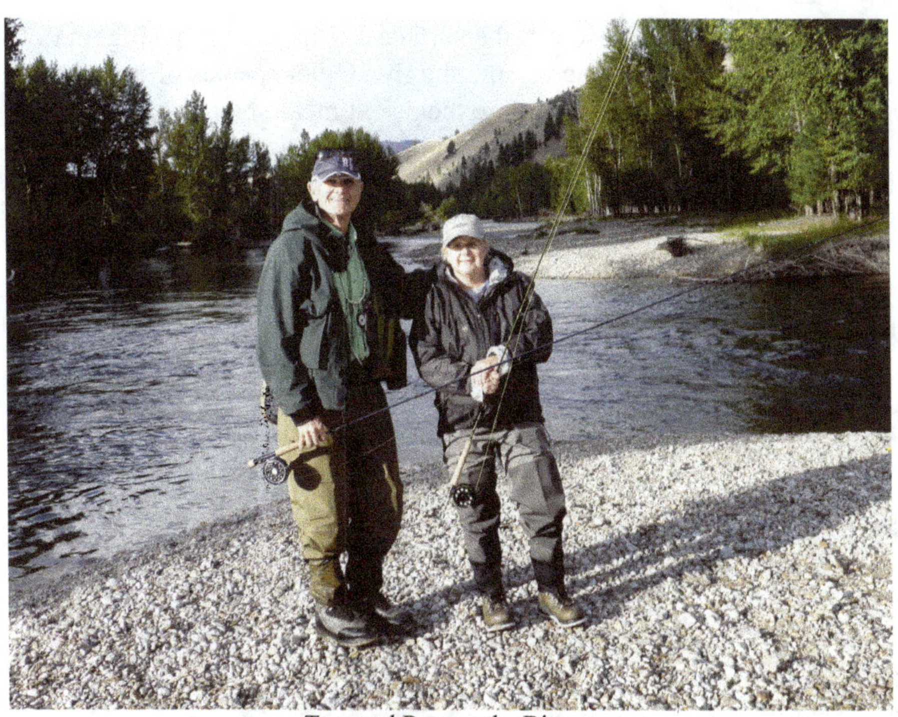
Tom and Pam on the Bitterroot

Elizabeth's prowess as an exceptional fly caster was obvious. Although she has only fly-fished a few times in the past, she's a quick learner and improviser. Being strong-willed and determined, coupled with innate athletic ability, she quickly mastered most of the basic fly rod casting techniques. With some guidance, Pam also became proficient with the over-the-shoulder, flip and role casting. The most difficult, but often the most captivating moments for the beginner, is learning about what tippet line size to use, and what type and size fly pattern might prove successful in any given number of circumstances. In the equation with this learning curve is the eye coordination of how to 'read a river', with presenting the fly at the proper depth to attract a wary trout. Regardless of the proficiency and knowledge that an angler processes, every venture forth presents a new and challenging set of circumstances. Knowing that we will never know it all as we anticipate the next pool around the bend, our interest grows and our eyes stay focused with anticipation and hope. Every bend in the river and each succeeding pool impose new challenges for the angler.

Fish were not rising for dries until early afternoon when a slight increase in temperature would trigger a hatch. We experimented with various flies on several sections of a most beautiful free-stone river, catching mostly small 12 to 16 inch cutthroats with an occasional rainbow obliging. Here and there 'window pockets' would appear where we could see feeding trout. With the right fly presentation into this mirror, a 'cuttie' would move slowly to the surface as if it were sneaking up to its quarry, and then with a quick burst, consume the fly. Other species of trout and salmon explode quickly to the surface to secure their next meal. Not so with the cutthroat. Often we would miss the 'take' by pulling the fly away before the fish could snatch it. One has to have veins of steel and the patience of Job to outwit the West's most widely-distributed native fish.

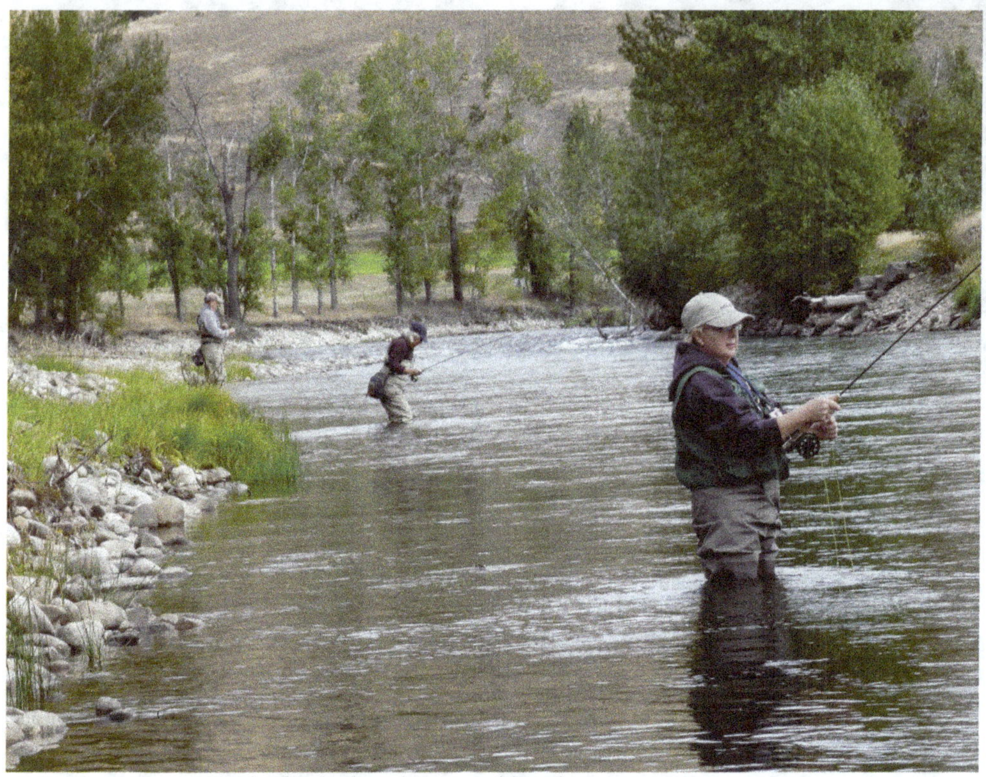
Ned, Elizabeth and Pam seeking the wary trout

With few trees along the banks to contend with, fly casting was easy except for intervals of wind blasts that would intermittently blow up and down the valley and intercept the direction of the cast. At this time of year grasshoppers are still active and we used small to medium-sized hoppers with effectiveness. Other types and sizes of flies that proved worthy were small dry tricos, midges, ants, elk hair caddis, and blue winged olives in sizes 16 to 22. The size and color of the hatch most often determined the size of the fly attached to the leader. I would sometimes use flies tied in tandem such as a hopper with a foot or so of leader attached to a smaller dry such as a trico. Wet flies also proved productive such as pheasant tails, prince nymphs, copper johns and bead-headed green or brown rib-bodied caddis. On occasion we brought to net hearty fish that slammed a wooly bugger, leech or streamer pattern.

Our second destination was the Wise River Club along the Big Hole River. We skipped into the corner of Idaho at one of the many places of traversing the 'great continental divide'. We took Chief Joseph Pass, and worked our way east along Route 43. This was rugged country of many sharp turns, steep grades and drops until it leveled off in the more pastoral valley setting in which we found the Big Hole National Battlefield.

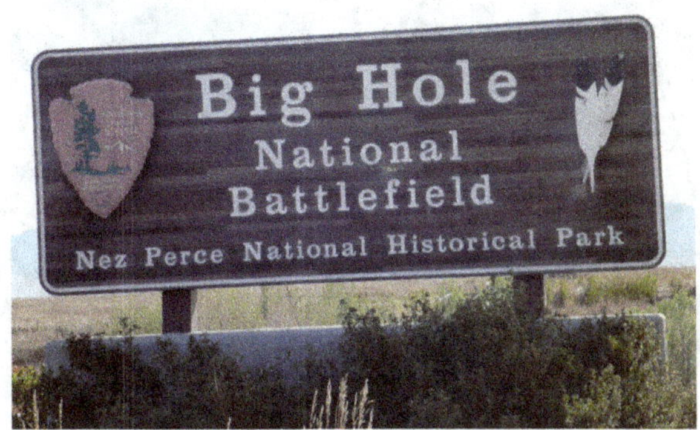

Here in the year 1877, the Nez Perce Indian's peaceful settlement along the upper flow of the Big Hole River was shattered by U.S. military forces who were under orders to remove the natives to a smaller reservation. Over 85 Nez Perce warriors, women and children were killed in this one of many bloody battles that plagued and scarred much of the West during these tumultuous years. The United State's large appetite to settle, manipulate and profit from the largess of natural resources including mining operations, led to many of these battles where numerous Indian tribes became uprooted, dispersed and killed by refusing to sign so-called 'treaties' drawn up by government officials. These atrocities and incursions into the lives of people who lived here for 3000 to 4000 years paint a nasty picture of the human race when it seeks power and dominance at any cost. It's the same old story played out countless times on our planet throughout recorded history—man's cruelty and heinous crimes against each other and particularly towards those ill equipped for defense and retaliation. I mention this tearful and retrospective interlude here in this meandering fishing narrative because the Nez Perce story in this majestic setting touched all of us in a profound way. Also it set the tone for our searching eyes seeking not only fish, but to acquiring knowledge of the West's past—both good and bad.

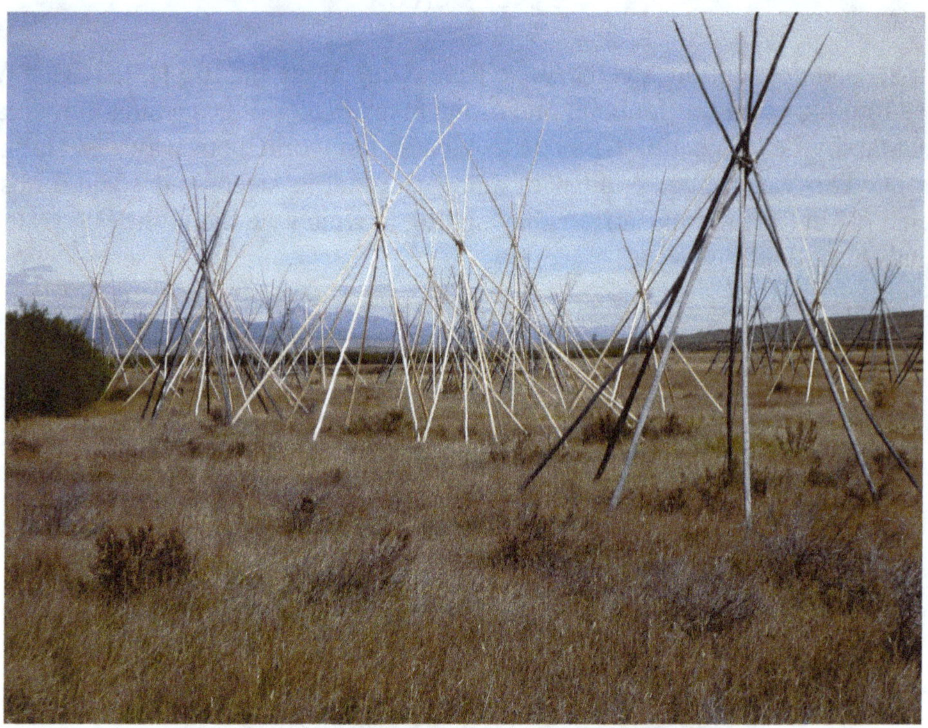

Nez Perce Teepees along the upper Big Hole River

We viewed the exhibit and walked along the now peaceful valley towards the original camping grounds of the Nez Perce with the north fork of the Big Hole River to our left. I carried my 2- weight fly rod along and from time to time would cast a caddis dry between the tall willows into a likely pool. Several rising trout spanked my fly while others just played with it as if it were a beach ball. I paused several times along the way and pictured the Indians fishing here with their spears and nets many moons ago. Pam, Ned and Elizabeth were getting ahead of me, so I hurried up the path to join them walking in these memorial grounds. Lodge pole pine teepees were erected at the same locations they were over 135 years ago. The names of the chiefs and important tribe members were displayed on tablets next to each teepee. We viewed this vast valley to the distant West Goat Peak Mountain Range and realized that it looked much the same as it did since the last ice age. You felt deep inside that you were on hallowed ground—a place of soulful peace and tranquility. Healing always takes time, and we all hoped it had come to this inspiring place along the banks of the famed Big Hole River.

Big Hole

Time was fleeing and we wanted to get in some fishing before the end of the day. So we hurried back to the car and continued our journey east to the town of Wisdom. We fueled up and meandered into the iconic Conover's Country Store.

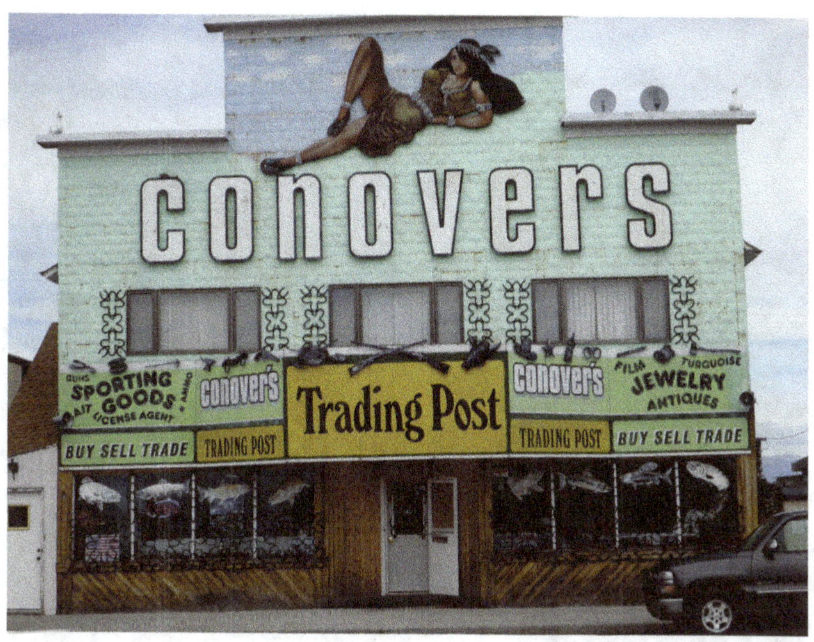

Not lacking for flies, Ned and I still couldn't resist buying a few more from the large selection on the counter. Departing again, we rounded the corner of the road where it comes in contact with Beaverhead Deerlodge National Forest and where the Big Hole River emerges out of the valley bigger and wider. A couple of fisherman came in view upstream where the road came close to the river. Peering over the river bank as we drove, we could see the water surface dimpling with the action of trout risings. "Wow guys, this river is alive with fish. There's a dry fly hatch going on. Let's pull over and get out our gear." We hurriedly came to an abrupt stop and popped up the trunk. Suitcases, groceries and various travel containers of all sorts soon littered the ground. Within a short time we slid down the banks where we all found solid casting ground on one of the large river rocks. The trout were rising to really small insects, and they would not touch my size 18 Caddis dry. Changing over to a size 22 Trico changed everything for the better. We lucked out with a Trico hatch of major proportions with literally hundreds of trout snorting the surface. The challenge and hope was to get a fish to hit your fly rather than the hundreds of real ones floating next to it. After many casts, several nice rainbows, browns and brook trout came to our waiting nets, until at last the hatch ended. Getting back into the car, we proceeded a few miles and found another large, long pool that we all could easily cast into. Here we caught larger rainbows and brookies on a variety of dries, including grasshopper patterns. It certainly turned into a magical afternoon. It satisfied our hopes to get in some fishing before the long shadows of the afternoon drew us into darkness.

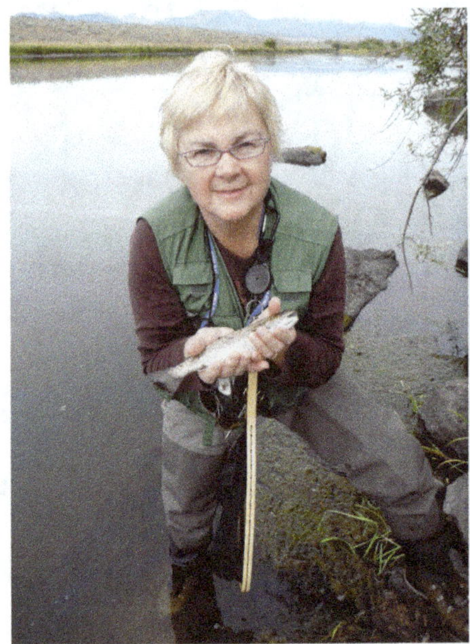
Pam at evening hatch

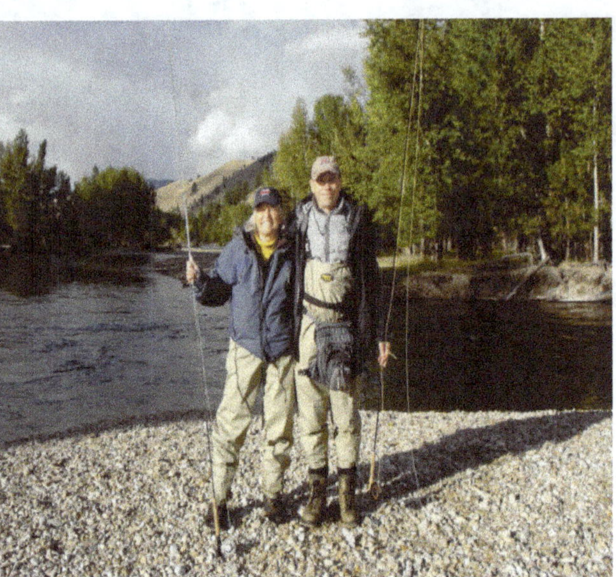
Elizabeth and Ned

Wise River

The next day we woke to a cool, crisp, wet morning at the rustic Wise River Club Hotel. Heavy rains had pelted our roof top all through the night and bans of fast-moving, diagonally-shaped dark clouds spilling rain were still hovering around us. After a hearty breakfast and several cups of coffee, we were off to fish a lower portion of the Big Hole, where we found several good locations following the road down to the town of Melrose. We found the fishing much tougher here. The water looked fine, but the barometer drop overnight might have had something to do with the fish turning off their appetites. In contrast, by the end of this day filled with wading and experimenting on many miles of river, our appetites were on the edge of being ravenous. Driving back to the club we noticed a dimly lit, pub-type diner. We pulled over and rambled in. Sitting around on bar stools with a circular table, we asked the waiter how the food was. "Well, ma mom is the cook and yer goin ta have ta be the judge of her cookin," was his reply. So playing it safe, we ordered up some sandwiches and some local, appetizingly named beer called Moose Droppings. All of our meals appeared salvageable, except for Elizabeth's so-called 'pork chop sandwich'. We all gazed at it as it sat steaming on her plate. It had a smoky-blackened glaze to it. Thinking the pork must be under this creasy glaze, Elizabeth began poking at it. As she spiked into it, nothing but hot air spewed out. We surmised that whatever pork there was before it was cooked had disappeared during the deep fry process. We all began to snicker. Pam, sitting just to the right, moved like a cat on the prowl. She screamed, "You're not eating that!" With one swoop of Pam's hand Elizabeth's plate flew off the table. In seconds Pam had cut her own sandwich in half, and slid it over to Elizabeth before she even had time to say ok. As Elizabeth sat motionless with an astonished look on her face at Pam's speedy determinism, we all burst into uncontrollable laughter. Ned and I came unglued off our chairs. "That was a repulsive-looking thing," Pam further exclaimed. We peered around to see if any of the other patrons were noticing Pam's fuss, when we spotted the cowboy sign over the back of the bar. It read: *Come In and Rest Your Weary Ass*. We burst out into laughter once again and my mind raced to find a way to enhance the signage with something more applicable. It came quickly as I sputtered, *"Come In With a Weary Ass and Leave with a Wearier One."* Well, that did it. Not being able to control our robust outbursts, and with a feeble attempt to not draw too much attention to us, we slid off our seats snickering through the front door. As soon as we felt safe outside under the overhanging roof, the night clouds let loose with torrential downpours that aided in camouflaging the laughing tears dropping from our cheeks. We left knowing that tonight's entertainment couldn't be duplicated again. For that we will be forever grateful.

Our next destination was the sleepy town of Cameron to fish the Madison River. On the way, we stopped in Dillon to get a bite to eat and to locate the Frontier Angler's Fly Shop. Elizabeth's boots were coming apart and new ones were in order. With all our gear re-checked and more new flies on our vest, we ventured over to view local sections of the Beaverhead River and the Poindexter Slough, a small, spring creek that eventually runs into the Beaverhead. Even though we hadn't planned on fishing here since we had many more miles to travel, the lure of the Poindexter flow was too much for us to pass up. This cool spring creek meanders slowly through meadows making for easy fly casting. However, since there was minimal cover along the banks, one had to go slow and low while casting to rising trout. The dimpling of trout mouths were everywhere. Fortunately, during the course of a couple hours, a few of the fish took our offerings on size 18 to 20 caddis dries. Most of the misses and netted trout were browns—native and wild. We could have easily fished here for a couple days, and it was difficult prying us off the river—next time I will surely stay longer.

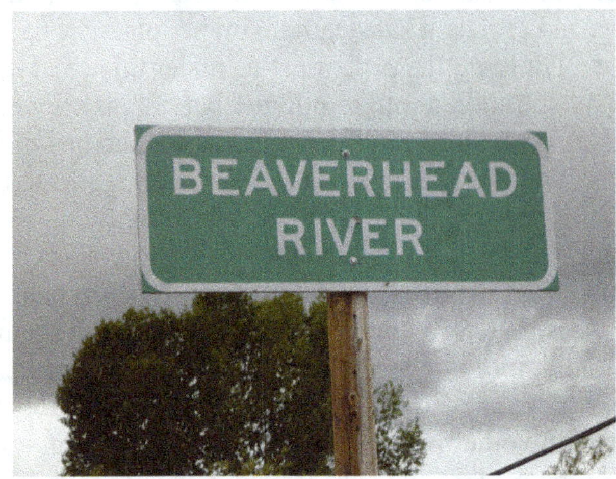

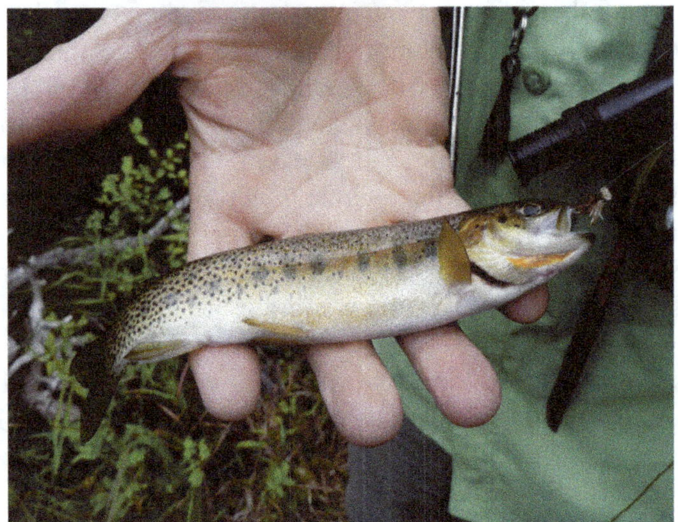

Small cuttie from small creek

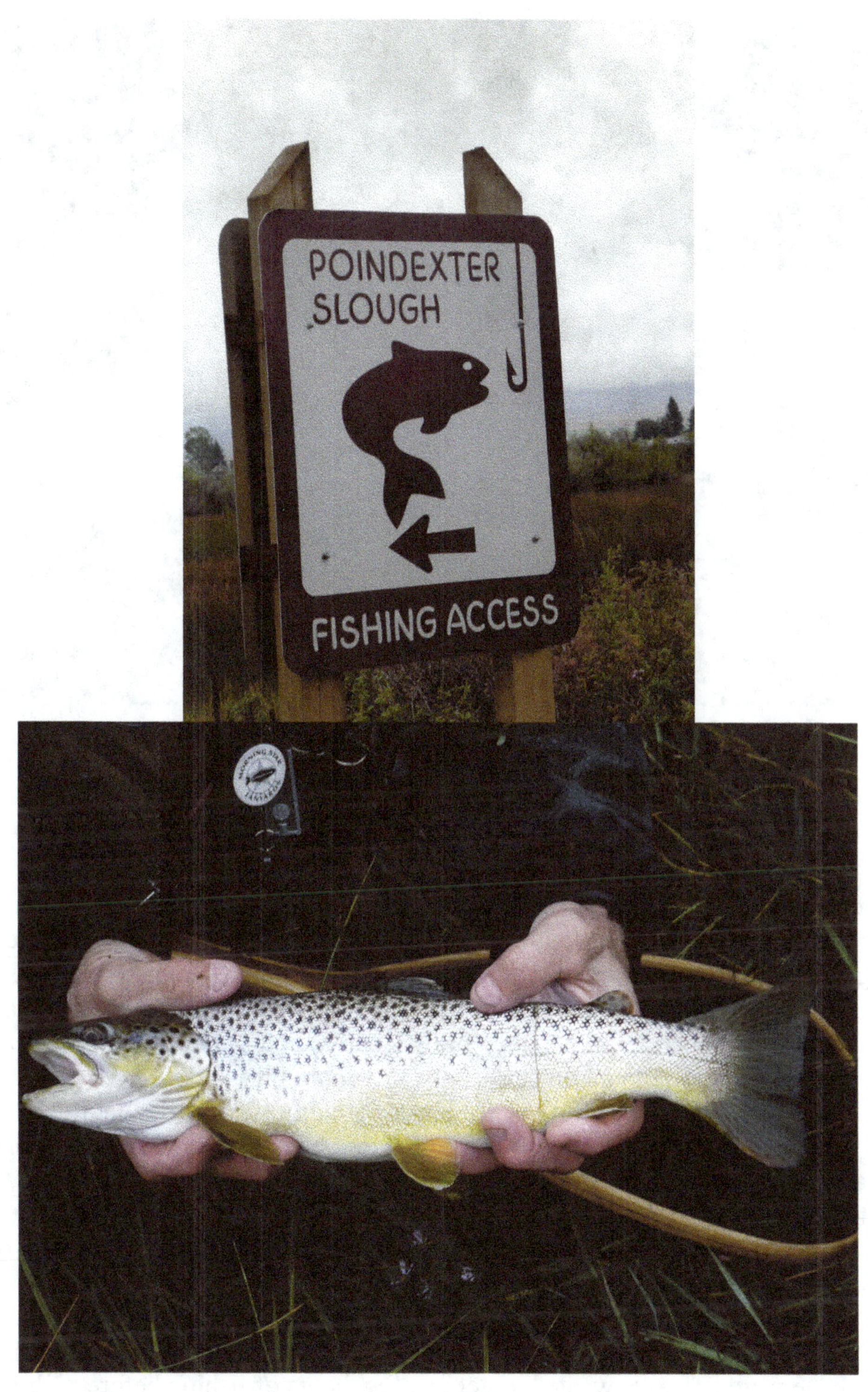

POINDEXTER
SLOUGH
FISHING ACCESS

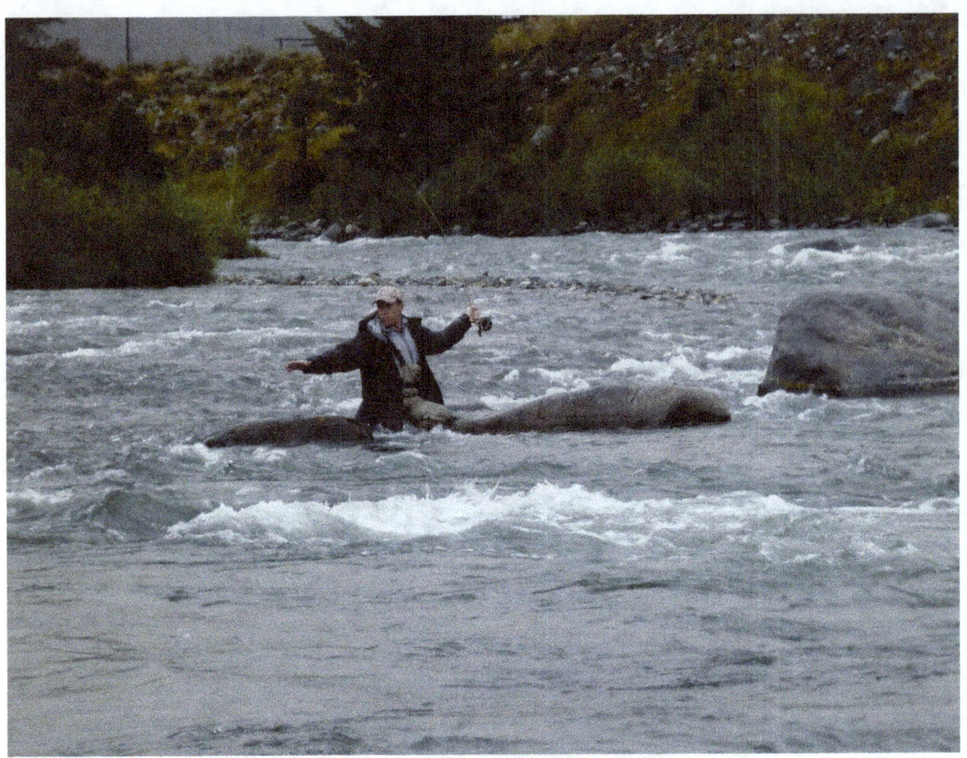

Ned playing a large brown trout while teetering on rocks

Centennial Valley

The rain clouds from the day before were still hanging around as we drove in and out of thunderheads. Ned recalled a remote, off-the-beaton-path dirt road that led through the Centennial Valley southeast along the Blacktail Road out of Dillon. It was a 50-mile jaunt through spectacular rolling country composed of green, lush, farmed valleys that married into matted brown, barren and sage-colored meadows surrounded by majestic mountain peaks. We saw more Pronghorn Sheep along this route than in any other in our travels. This was certainly 'Big Sky' at its finest. Early weather-beaten 19th century settler homes and barns were scattered here and there alongside the rolling valley road. Finally we came to Red Rocks Lakes National Refuge and viewed the Trumpeter White Swan Restoration Project at the ranger station's display room. This is a majestic 49,906 acre refuge with over 16,000 acres of lakes and marshes that provide restorative habitat for many bird and mammal species. Proceeding east along the Idaho border to our south, we came up over Red Rock Pass heading north into Cameron. It was a long day of travel and although we were tired, we wanted to get in a few hours of fishing before nightfall. We slid into the Slide Inn along the banks of the Madison. With only a few hours of light left, our fly rods went quickly into action as we spread out along the river just below the inn. After a day of rain, the river was higher than usual. With cool temperatures and roiling waters, I opted for a heavy, dark wooly bugger presentation to get the fly down into the hitting zone. Casting up and over several large river rocks that led into a wide, deep-cut pool, a fish finally latched onto the fly after several across-the-shoulder maneuvers. I could tell it was the largest and strongest fish I had hooked so far on the trip and after several strong runs and swirls, a nice fat 18 inch brown trout came to net.

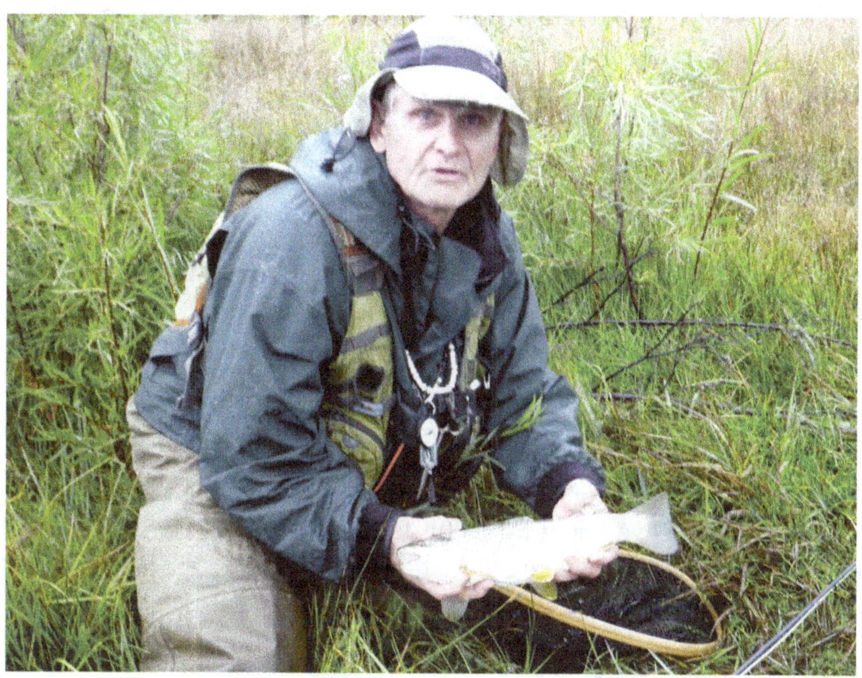

Ned also had tied into several nice fish above me as he was teetering on a rock midstream between several likely holding spots. It looked like he was struggling to stay afoot against the turbulent, swirling waters, and I kept my eye on him just in case he needed assistance—for surely he would have floated by me quickly if he lost his balance. I watched him as he netted a large, leaping rainbow. After a quick release we both gave a thumbs up. The girls were fishing below us and caught several browns and rainbows that were hiding behind rocks and undercuts near the river's banks.

Chapter 5

Yellowstone

America's oldest and most spectacular national park beckoned us. We had waited until September before venturing here to avoid much of the clatter and clamor of too many cars and cameras on too few roads. Entering through the West Yellowstone entrance, we followed the Madison River to the town of Madison. From here it was south along the Firehole River to the Old Faithful Inn for lunch and a short tour of the visitors center. We had to pinch ourselves several times on route with the urge to fish the appealing stretches of river that we viewed while passing by. Proceeding west to Grant Village there is a sharp bend north along the picturesque Yellowstone Lake to the junction at Fishing Bridge. Continuing north along the Yellowstone River, the famous Upper and Lower waterfalls came into view. Their splendor of force, size and color against the canyon walls was something a picture or a painting could never do justice to. These superlative vistas carved out by nature over the eons have to be seen with the naked eye to truly be appreciated and admired. Many animals were photographed as we drove along—bison, elk, coyotes and pronghorn sheep were plentiful. One she-wolf was viewed at a distance just once as we heard the howls of wolves on a slope just above her. Heading north still further, we finally came into the vast, untamed Lamar Valley following the Lamar and Soda Creek streams up into the northeast park entrance. Although there are sparse accommodations inside the park, we opted for a comfortable cabin just outside of the park in Cooke City. There are several adequate rustic places to stay here as well as in the neighboring town of Silver Gate.

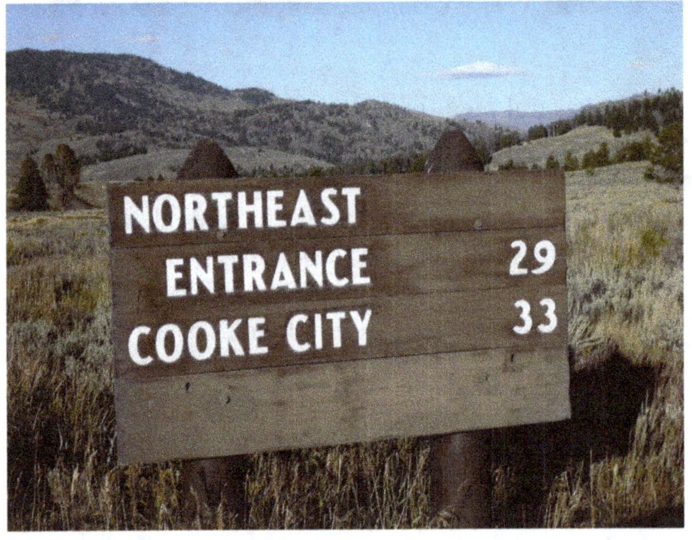

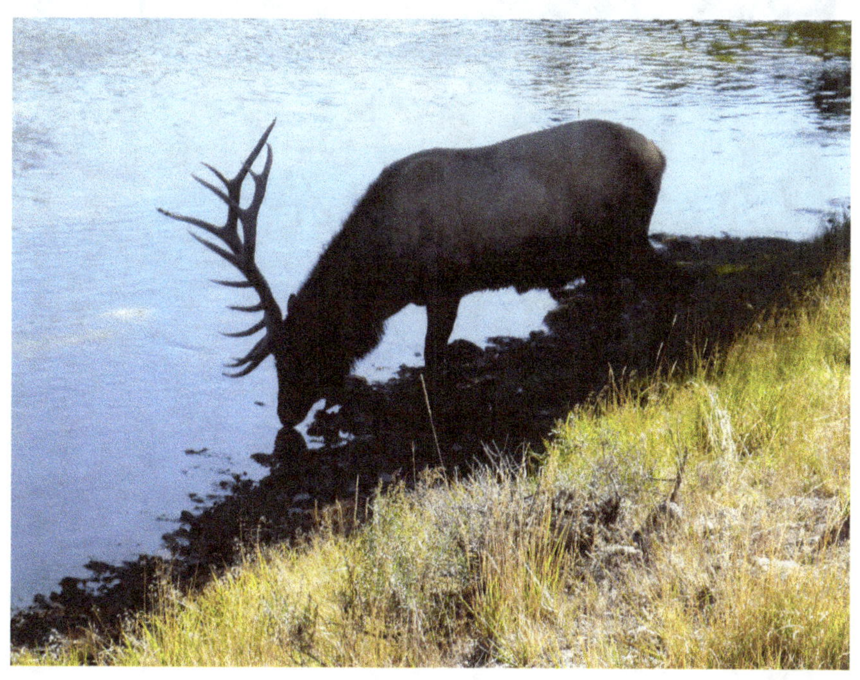

For the next few days we fished several small creeks in the northeast sector of the park. We found the best overall fishing here. We hiked up and down Slough Creek, finding upper meadows filled with cutthroats up to 20 inches. The mornings were cool, but as the sun got higher in the early afternoon, it warmed up into the 70's and the trout began to hit grasshoppers and beetles. The larger Lamar River, which follows much of the road bisecting the northeast sector of the park, provided the most consistent fish- taking pools with many eager cutthroats smashing small wets and dry flies. Prior to the great action on the Lamar, I hooked into one fish in a moiling, short slot of a sulfur-smelling section of the Yellowstone River just below where the Lamar River merges into it. Wading along up and over boulders and pebble strewn sections, many animal bones were exposed—whitened spikes sticking up along the river banks, reminding us of how wild, pure and special this place is on earth.

> *"We know all too much about how to fish and vastly too little*
> *about what it means to fish..."*

> ~Verlyn Klinkenborg (1993)

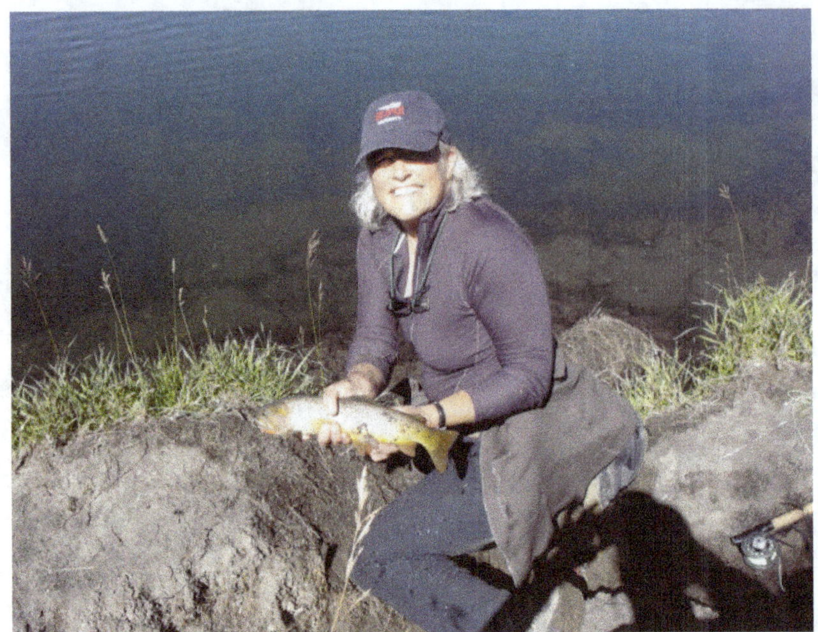

Elizabeth with one of her larger cutthroats on Slough Creek

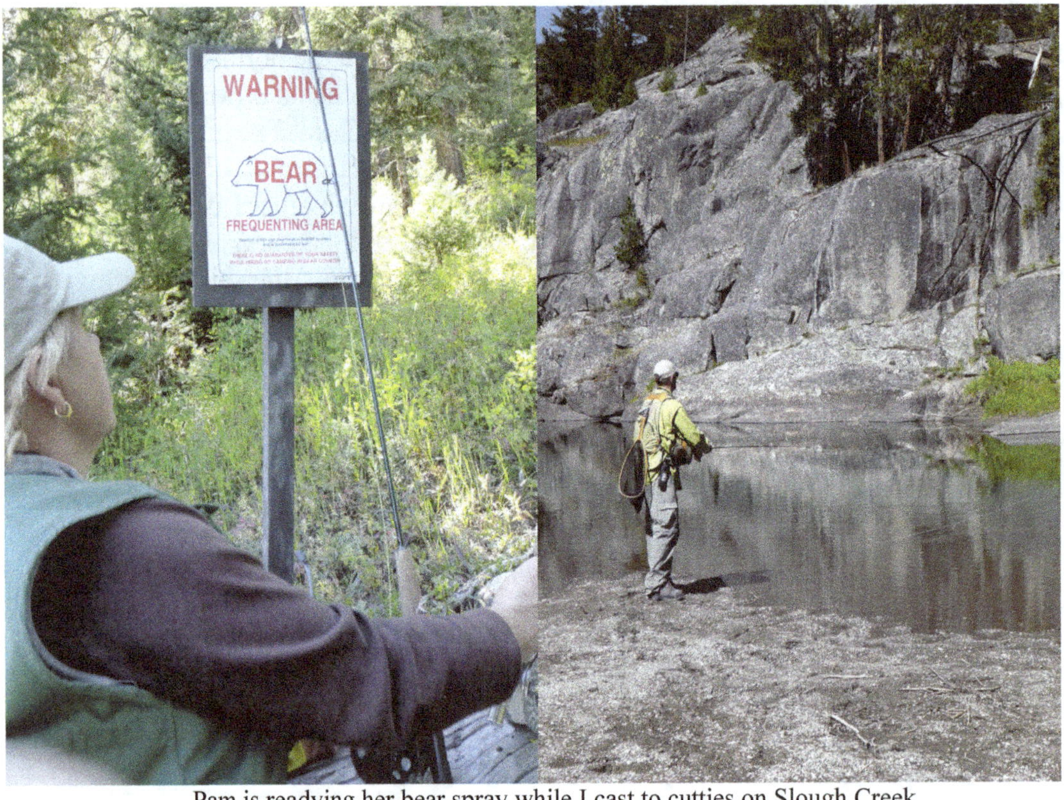

Pam is readying her bear spray while I cast to cutties on Slough Creek

Chapter 6

Henry's Fork and Beyond

Our last three days of fishing were reserved at The Angler's Lodge along the banks of the famous Henry's Fork River. Ned and Elizabeth showed us many great sections to fish along this long and diverse river. We primarily fished the Box Canyon area and a lower run from the Warm River to Ashton. Pam and I enjoyed a float trip on two long river sectors, and with the help of the guide, she learned much about nymph presentation, hooking up, line tension and reeling in. We caught a combination of rainbows, whitefish and the occasional large sucker. It was surprising how well the suckers fought—they did not come in too easily. Any fish that smashes a fly and gives a gamely fight is written in my next book as a game fish—in this case a very determined, primitive bottom-sucking fighter.

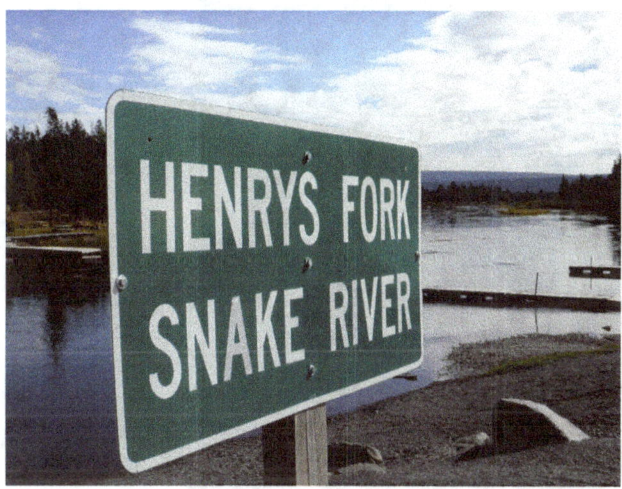

One morning in the Canyon section of the river, Pam was downstream from me; Ned and Elizabeth were up river. All you could hear was the gentle flow of the river when suddenly out of this quiet we heard Pam scream out at the top of her lungs. I jumped up on the bank, slipped over a couple boulders to look downstream to find out what was the matter. Pam was motoring along up towards me still screaming, "Tom it's a rat! A rat! A big black rat! Eeeeaaaukk!" As she came up to me, I grabbed her quivering arm and helped her get up on the bank. Her face was flush with total disgust and fright. "What was it honey?"

"Tom, I was fishing and just looked down at my boots and saw a squirmy, black rat swimming in between my boots. It freaked me out! Yuck!"

"Pam, it's not a rat. It's a muskrat. They won't hurt you." I started to chuckle, and Pam was not amused. She had banged her knee on a rock trying to escape from the river rat, so we rested on the river bank nursing her pain while Ned and Elizabeth came down to find out what happened. They first thought that Pam was hurt only to find out that her mind was bewildered from the ordeal of the moment. Sitting and musing a while to build up our strength and composure, we talked about how many miles we had traveled and walked, the rivers we had fished and the magnificent exposure we had to the great scenery of the West. Pam was now broken in as a fly fisher—certainly in more ways than one. She was as eager as me to fish as often and as long as we could, going all day long until exhaustion and darkness came to reprieve us. It's a workout—one of the best mental and physical workouts known to man.

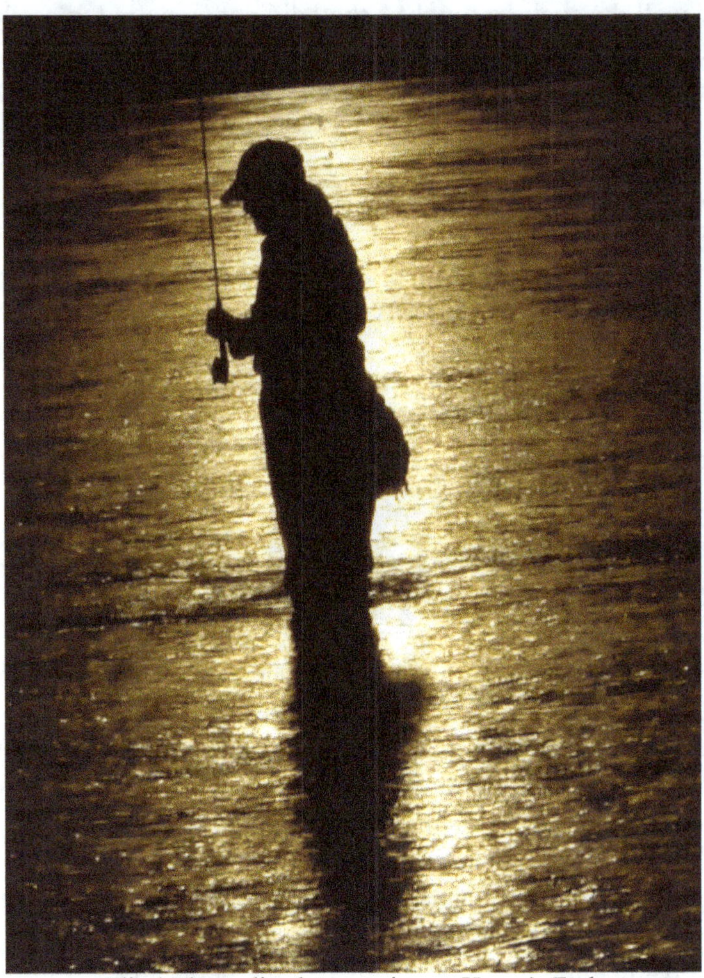

Elizabeth treading late evening on Henry's Fork

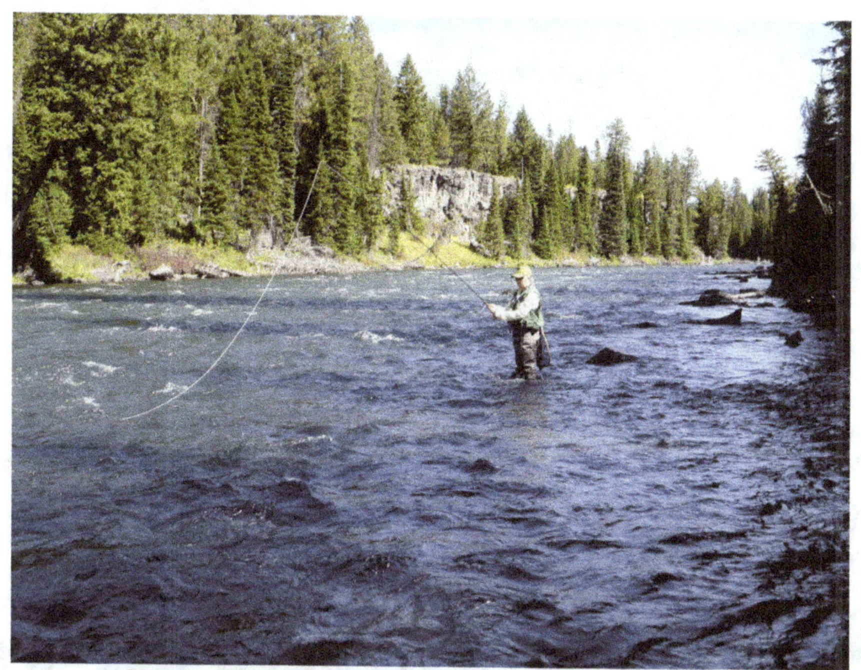

Pam navigating Box Canyon prior to muskrat attack

A few months prior to planning this western trek, Pam announced, to my surprise, that she wanted to get into fly fishing. Although she had fished with me intermittently in the past, she had never taken it seriously. She was now ready to take on a new hobby and open herself up to her husband's favorite pastoral sport. This was her first extended fishing excursion with friends that are seasoned outdoor people, who will go anywhere for rugged adventure and fun. Just as it proved skiing with them in the past, Ned and Elizabeth kept us on the go climbing up and down canyon walls and walking for miles to find remote fishing spots. We started early each morning and got off the rivers at dusk. Pam amazingly kept up with us, with always an open eye to learning and experimenting. There were a few remote trails we took with bear-warning signs that Pam did not take a liking to. I assured her that with our belted bear spray, any bear that got too close would be repelled with the eye-burning misty bombs. "Ya sure," Pam would mordantly reply, not really convinced that these little bear-repellent bottles would actually work. I was delighted with Pam's gutsiness and determination, all with less down-time than she's accustomed to. She toughed it up, roughed it up and opened herself up to the joys, frustrations and amusements of fly fishing. I am more than proud of my favorite girl.

"The angling fever is a very real disease and can only be cured by the application of cold water and fresh, untainted air."

~Theodore Gordon

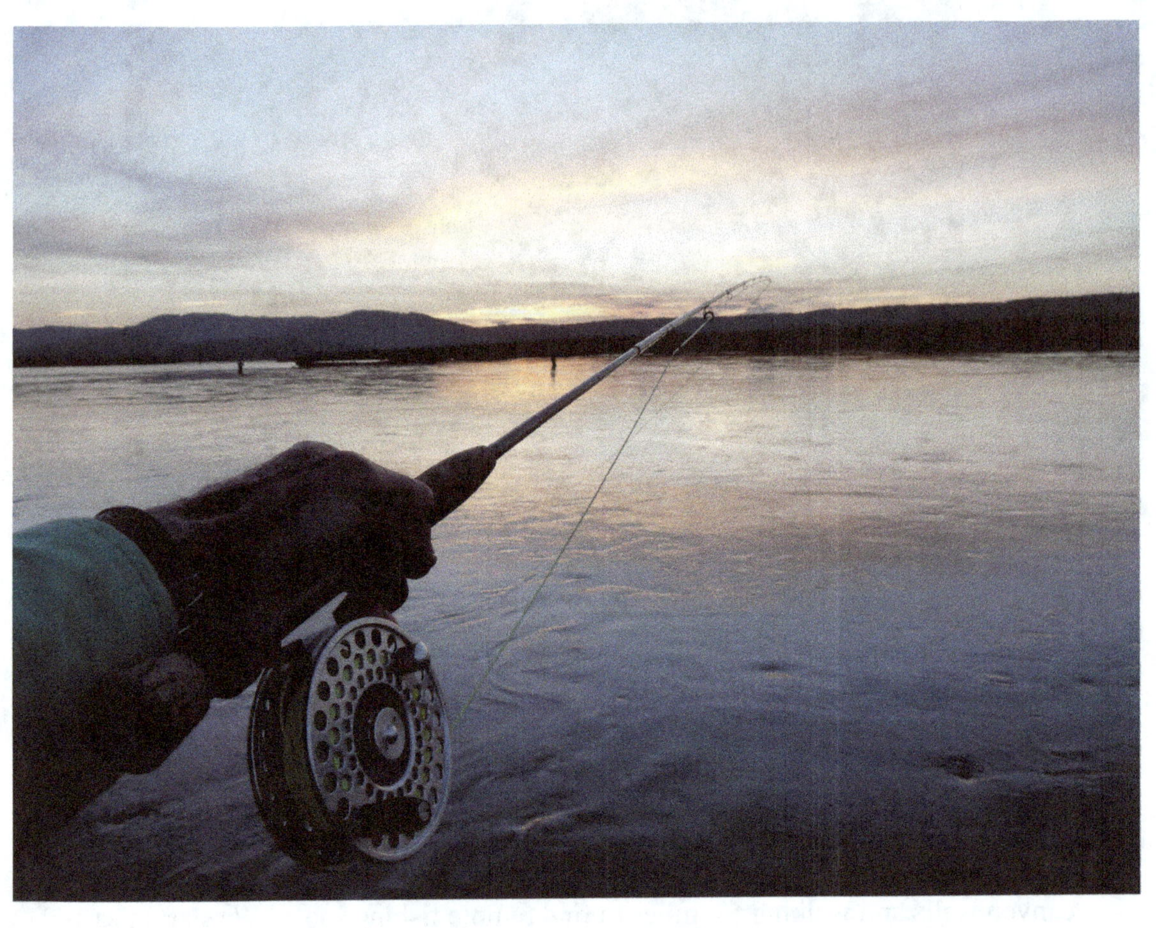

Chapter 7

Epic Bow Hunt

Hunting with the bow and arrow in a territory where there are healthy numbers of deer has many benefits. These benefits are maximized with many other blessings forthcoming when the area you hunt hasn't been disturbed by too many hunters or predators. With proper scouting and some know how, the sportsman will have certain success year in and year out. I've hunted whitetails in all of the New England states for over 45 years—first using wooden long bows and arrows before graduating to recurves and compounds. For the past few years, Maine has become my favorite place to pursue America's favored big- game animal.

October is a magical and wholesome time to be in the woods. Many days begin with frosty cool mornings giving way to penetrating, warm sun. Other days, light rains dampen the leaves that have been chased by the wind. Squirrels frantically harvest and store their larder of oak nuts for the harsh winter ahead. The smell of drifting leaves mixed with the faint aroma of spruce permeate the nostrils, as one's eyes fix themselves on the mix-colored landscapes. Yes, the rich and vivid sights and scents of autumn are intoxicating to all who venture forth. After a few icy nights and leaf-falling, the woods open up as deer begin to attack acorns and apples. Prior to the real cold weather coming, the temperature is comfortable, the woods are quiet and the deer are not yet in the alert mode. Such was the case in the fall of 2010, but the unfolding hunt was surprisingly more special than many of the past.

Two years ago after the hunting season had closed, I was scouting the internal forested area of one of my favorite peninsulas along the coast. It was the first time I had taken my ATV so deep in these woods down a rugged, jagged-edged logging road. Coming up over a crest in four inches of newly fallen snow, two white tails came into and out of view in what seemed like a second. It was as if I was viewing a speeded up film of super large bunny tails jumping through the snow-laden pines, leaving white-puffed crystals falling in their wake. Soon I saw many tracks going in every direction across this knob. To my rear was a small swamp. To my front was a thicket of spruce. To my left and right were oak and maple hardwoods interspersed with laurels and small saplings. Several deer runs came together where the old logging road melted away down the further slope. Best yet, there were buck rubs on several saplings and rutting scrapes under a few low-hanging spruce limbs. After circling and semi-circling the area for over an hour, I found a spruce tree that I could affix a tree stand to that would give me the best location, height and concealment needed for some future hunt.

Two hunting seasons later, I was finally on my way to this stand. You may ask: why did I wait so long? Well, this is big woods—particularly for bow hunting. Deer are 'animals of the edges', and I had hunted successfully 'pinch points' nearer apple trees and fields that were not far from the main roads of my house. With venison in the freezer, most of my hunting was over by mid October. Also, in my mind, I thought this was a better gunning stand due to its location so deep in the woods with distant shooting lanes up to 100 yards or more. For some reason this year, the stands that proved productive in the past were not working out.

I was in no hurry to get up early that day in late October. I prepared my backpack for a lengthy stay in the woods at a tree stand that I hoped was still in good shape. After ATVing to within 150 yards of the location, I scented up and walked slowly to the stand—gingerly climbing up into the seat by 10:00 am. The day was overcast with virtually no wind and the ground was damp after a previous day of light rain. The conditions were perfect. As my bow hung on a nearby branch, my head became that of an owl—turning around constantly, searching for any movement or sound. I had no idea what direction a deer might come poking through. After twenty minutes of sitting and standing quietly, it was time to make some noise. About every half hour or so, I mixed in buck grunts and rattling. I made sure that the rattling started off slowly and lightly, ending with much banging and intensity. If possible, I hoped a distant buck would hear this orchestrated fight between two of his rivals. At 11:50 am I spotted the movement of something brown coming through the front thicket of spruce. Grey squirrels were running and digging in this area all morning, and at first I thought it might just be one bigger-than-usual bush tail. I stood up, grabbed my bow, and sure enough, the brown spot became a deer. It was walking slowly, cautiously and directly towards me. It stopped 30 yards to my left behind trees, turned right as its rack came into view, and proceeded to walk broadside at 20 yards. It was a silent entrance onto the main stage in front of me, as the buck boldly entered on moist, soft, mossy ground. If I was looking in another direction I would have never seen him. My dad had reminded me many years ago: "Tom, you have to be alert at all times. These cagey creatures come and go like ghosts in the wind—especially when they are sneaking cautiously with all their senses on high alert."
Having no time to think (thankfully) or get too many jitters (who doesn't), I drew back and let the broadhead fly. The buck whirled around and beat a ticket across the logging road to the other side of the swamp. It was 12 noon. For ten minutes or so I saw nothing except where the deer had disappeared, and then I saw it fall. Evidently the deer proceeded into the swamp, stopped, and did a semi-circle back and expired within eyesight. I said to myself, "You got to be kidding me! Yes! Thank you, Lord! Could anything be better than this? Wow!" I sat still savoring the moment, and trying to recover some semblance of composure for twenty minutes. There was no need to hurry, and I wanted to relish this interlude in the silence of these woods. I

had all day, and it's always best to make sure the game is down for good. I learned early on in my junior years that 'jumping' a wounded deer is never a good idea. Many animals are never found by hunters who are too quick to get on the trail—even those deer that they see go down and think are dead sometimes get up and bound away. Haste most often only leads to waste.

After retrieving my arrow sunk deep in the moss, I walked slowly across the edge of the swamp with a second arrow corked in the bow just in case another shot was needed. Within 8 yards of the deer, I stopped and just admired him. I propped the 7-point buck in between two trees, cleaned it and then proceeded to drag it 30 yards to the logging trail. Backing up the ATV into a gully, I rolled the buck onto the game carrier, holding it on with bungee cords. The thick chocolate-colored rack was perfectly symmetrical. I estimated the hoof weight at 200 lbs. Not a huge buck, but not a small buck either—just a perfectly healthy 2 and a half to 3 year old prime-of-his-life buck that would provide healthy eating for the next several months. It was the end of a memorable and epic hunt. Not a hard hunt. On the contrary, it was an easy one. It could very well be described as just a lucky day. Nevertheless, it was certainly a planned hunt that was thought out two years before my first visit to this magical stand.

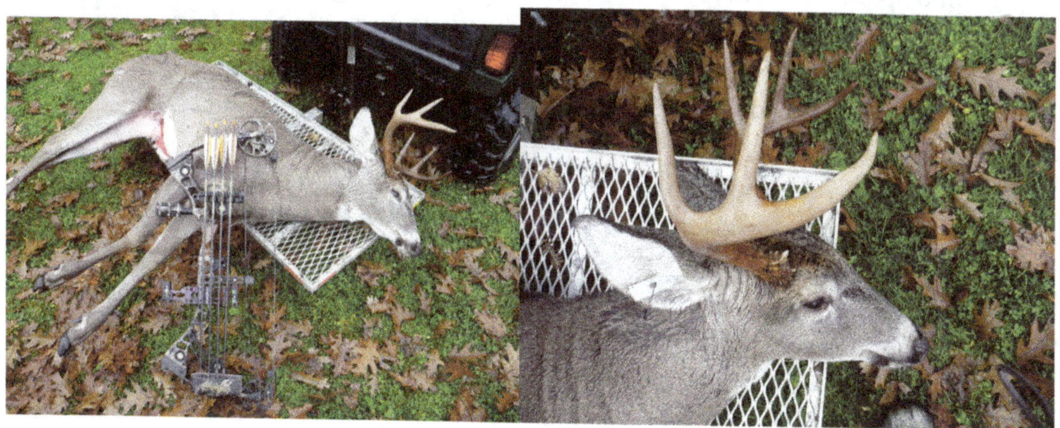

There are at least three important lessons for the hunter here that come to mind. First, scouting and placing the right stand location is a prerequisite to success—most importantly for a bow hunter. Secondly, depending upon the topography and general characteristics of the area, the tree stand needs to be at the proper height off the ground. If the stand is placed too low, an approaching deer may spot or smell you.

Hoof pounding, a chorus of snorts and bolting jumps could be the end result of a poorly placed stand. I generally like a stand placement 25 to 30 ft. off the ground, preferably in an evergreen tree such as a spruce that will hide my outline. Often, in this position, my scent will carry above the ground far enough so a deer can't whiff my location. Another major advantage is being able to slowly move into position to shoot without being detected. Thirdly, learning and applying the natural sounds of deer adds measurably to the result of any hunt. Rattling, principally induced during pre-rut and even into early November, often moves bucks in your direction. Last year, after rattling on and off for an hour or so, three bucks bounded out from my left down a runway and stopped 25 yards directly in front of my tree stand. It wasn't a matter of missing the shot (although it's happened) since the deer were so close; it was just a matter of what buck did I want to shoot. Often in late September and through October, bucks will hang out together before the urge of mating takes over, when their natural, instinctive inclination directs them to pursuing estrus does and becoming rivals.

   This year's late October hunt will not be lost to my own memory. I undoubtedly will tell and re-tell this tale to my grandchildren, and maybe someday they will share with their children the story of great Grampa's epic hunt in the Maine woods. This is certainly what memories are made for. Also, these recollections and storytelling help to bind sportsman together and keep our great hunting traditions alive and well. I always count each day a special blessing when I venture into the Maine woods to hunt and fish.

Chapter 8

The Heart of a Hunter

What is the heart of a true hunter? The majority of sportsman pursuing deer and all wild game share much in common, with their first genuine concern centered on the health and welfare of the animals they are seeking. I emphasize and differentiate the word 'sportsman' from those who just hunt for meat and those who have no regard for the welfare of others or of the game they are pursuing. I was brought up in a fishing and hunting family who taught me about the woods, the waters and the wild inhabitants therein. As paradoxical as it may appear on the surface to many non-hunters, seekers of native game work in conjunction with their local fish and game departments to establish laws that benefit the habitat and overall well-being of those animals and birds that they hunt, and they put up the monies to pay for conservation initiatives. Nationwide, deer, moose, elk and bear populations have soured over the past decade to record numbers. The same can be said about turkeys and the ruffed grouse.   It is a well-known fact that hunting helps to keep the population of wild game in check and aids in establishing a healthier and more robust herd or flock. Sportsmen's monies are largely responsible for the resurgence of the native wild turkey to our landscape, particularly in New England, over the past 25 years. Certain critical areas such as lands in close proximity to villages, towns and cities or sectors of limited terrain such as islands, are often given special status as 'expanded hunting zones' that allow archery hunting only. The general population and the health of the deer are put at risk if too many animals are congregated in too close proximity to neighborhoods and relocated to small sections of land. Deer carrying Lyme disease is a major concern and health issue. One blatant example of rapid lime infections which posed a real threat to the health and welfare of the people occurred off the Maine coast on Monhegan Island a few years ago. Many residents became deathly sick from the bite of deer ticks carrying the dreaded disease. It became so bad that all of the deer on the small island had to be eradicated to prevent an epidemic and to also protect the fragile plant life that the rising deer population were feasting on.

So where is the heart of the hunter? Hunters are called upon to promote conservation and preservation initiatives for all our wild native animals that have been sought after by Americans for many generations. Traditions run deep in many families including my own. Unwittingly, we help with the needed funding with purchases of licenses, gear and, for many, lodging. It is important to protect and stand up for our hunting freedoms, and the second amendment. We must do what is necessary to protect our deep-rooted customs and outdoor way of life. It is equally important to promote hunting with all outdoor groups and organizations as a conservation tool that works for the benefit of all wildlife and habitat. Most men and women who feel the way I do are simply drawn to the beauty and bounty that awaits them in the wilds of forests that are comprised of multiple types of challenging terrain and magnificent scenery. We are called by nature to participate with it on its raw and uncompromising terms. We wouldn't want it any other way. There is a sense of peace, satisfaction and relaxation that comes to one when they are immersed deep in the woods, on mountain tops or walking stealthily around the edges of hidden swamps and bogs. We have an ancient, innate physical connection to the natural world resulting in a spiritual link that goes to the core of our beings. The heart of a hunter is centered on the anticipation, the journey, the challenge and the quest — not the kill. The ultimate luxury is when one is fortunate enough to tag an animal or bird, and enjoy the treat of feasting on meat that is free from hormones, chemicals and store labels.

Notwithstanding, there are anti-hunting groups that state that hunting is "barbaric and unnecessary" for wildlife management. They point to contraceptive techniques and other so-called 'progressive' procedures to keep animal populations in check. Attempts at controlling wild game populations vis-à-vis artificial contraceptive procedures are futile at best, and are most often expensive and not cost effective. Seventy five percent of Americans approve of hunting, and I include in this book many reasons why wild game is fun to pursue and tasty and healthy to eat. It is also much less costly to manage game populations when sportsmen are involved in the equation. Manually applied contraceptive procedures can run into millions of dollars and often these so-called anti-hunting advocate groups target one species, while ignoring others that also require management. Their playing field is never level and they purposely ignore the facts behind tried and true conservation measures and successes. There are a host of organizations that exist for the purpose of trying to take away other's freedoms. They masquerade around expounding nonsense about how their only care and concern is for the poor animals or wild forests that are being exploited by hunters, fisherman and industry. Their energies are most often misplaced with words and acts that are based on misconceptions and falsehoods devoid of scientific and statistical facts.

Fortunately there are groups such as the National Rifle Association (NRA) that continue to fight for our second amendment rights and those of sportsman. Although I don't agree with everything the NRA expounds upon, where else can I find a committed organization that will defend our right to bare arms? On the federal government level there appears to be a growing disconnect between policy makers and the 10 million Americans that hunt. Hunters are willing and able to manage any lands where the population of animals becomes too large for the land to handle. They should have been put to good service on Santa Rosa Island off the coast of California. Instead, a century-old iconic population of Roosevelt elk and Kaibab mule deer were slaughtered in late December, 2011 by our very own National Park Service, who employed sharpshooters to do the dirty work. Virtually no one knows about this episode since the national media didn't hone in on its importance and catastrophic bloody results. Where were they? It is understandable that a small island over time would become overpopulated with game with no natural predators, and that the ecosystem of that island could be put in jeopardy. Over the course of the last decade or so, hunters could have been given special permits to manage wildlife, which has led to healthier herds, without decimating the entire animal population. The massacre killing of these magnificent island animals is a tragedy of massive proportions. The island could still manage to harbor sizable herds of elk and mule deer. Why were they all killed? Where is the public outcry? Where were our comatose elected officials to stop such ill-advised, publically-funded federally mandated blunders?

Just to the south of Santa Rosa is the island of Catalina which has a healthy population of 150 to 200 bison. The Catalina Island Conservancy states that these bison are "a heritage herd woven into the island's cultural and economic fabric." To manage the herd, contraceptive techniques are employed at a cost of $175,000 annually. Gun and/or archery hunters would gladly pay license fees to support the conservancy and save them this money by culling the herd whenever the population rose to levels that posed a problem to the island. For some reason the conservancy does allow hunting on the island for wild hogs and mule deer, probably with the belief that ridding the island of competitors helps the bison. Certainly hogs are notorious for ruining the landscape and fragile island ecosystems. Why don't they include bison hunting in this trilogy? The extremist anti-hunting group called In Defense of Animals (IDA) was involved in saving the buffalo on Catalina. Curiously and perplexingly, they seemingly ignored the slaughter that occurred on nearby Santa Rosa. Was it because the killings were not done by nondescript hunters, or was their organization paid to keep their mouths shut? Isn't it their function to stop the killing of animals, or, in retrospect, is their only true function that of just being against hunting? Why weren't the Santa Rosa elk and mule deer also considered "truly woven into the island's cultural and economic fabric?" In fact, their pedigree was stronger since they were there at least 14 years before the bison were introduced on Catalina in 1926.

The bottom line is that all federal and state agencies responsible for the conservation and preservation of our native wildlife should employ the use of our hunting traditions that have been in place since the country was founded. Hunting organizations do not want to eradicate species — rather they desire to preserve them and keep the cycle of life healthy for future generations to enjoy. Hunting has been stooped in our heritage and economic fabric for over 250 years. As such, it is an integral part of our cultural fabric. Now that's what I call a founding father's tradition and institution that should be admired and built upon by all our natural resource agencies rather than being diminished by them. These roots go deep, and we need to remember and promote our pedigree by utilizing our sportsman's talents and voices for the enhancement of our environment. Something is amiss within the makeup and decision making of our National Park Service. Whom do they serve? More sportsmen need to speak up and engage their elected officials and local media so that these injustices are brought to light and corrected. Let's engage sportsman in all environmental concerns so that their services and expertise can be used in balancing decision making processes. In doing so we could save the taxpayer millions of dollars that are now being spent foolishly and inappropriately.

Pittman-Robertson Act

To further acerbate the frustrations that sportsman face, the Pittman-Robertson Federal Aid in Wildlife Restoration Funding program has been mismanaged and misused for decades. Since 1939 this wildlife enhancement funding has been allocated to all states that can match the monies with 25% in state matching funds. This aid is made possible by a 11% federal excise tax on guns, ammunition and bows and arrows (10% for handguns). The act dictates that the currency be used only for "wildlife habitat preservation and restoration" to help insure healthy populations of wildlife and ultimate successful hunting. Are hunters being rewarded for what they are being taxed for? How is the money being spent? In Maine, like most states, the money route has lost its compass and purpose. The majority of funds are being filtered over to salaries and operating costs in an effort to keep the Fish and Game Department afloat and to fund non-habitat projects such as research, culvert/bridge/ building construction, trail maintenance, and dock/float installations etc. Since 1939 Maine has received more than $60 million ($4.5 million alone in 2010). Yet only a small portion of these funds have or are being used to enhance wildlife habitat. Early in the 20th century 70-80 % of our land consisted of early-successional habitat, with the balance being made up of 20-30 % mature forest. Today, particularly in New England, about 80% of the land has reversed to mature forest growth. In order to maintain and nourish all native wildlife species, these forests would require a 30-50% reduction through timber harvesting and other reduction measures. In Maine, tree harvesting, field mowing and related enhancement work has only been done on approximately 2,000 acres of the total Wildlife Management Area (WMA) holdings. It is further disturbing to note that these Maine lands are enjoyed by many other types of recreational users, such as bikers, snowmobilers, cross-country skiers, ATV operators, and hikers who benefit from these hunter-generated dollars. The bottom line is that the hunter gains little, while all other outdoor enthusiasts benefit greatly. Much alarm has been made about the depleting numbers of deer in northern Maine counties. Most of the blame has been attributed to harsh winters and coyote kills, but we must add one more contributing factor—the dire lack of forest and field restoration practices that are beneficial to enhancing wildlife and, in particular, deer and game bird habitat.

What can be done to get these hunter-taxed dollars into circulation for what they were intended by law to accomplish—to profit better wildlife habitat, rather than having these funds being siphoned into general recreation and other non-descript uses? It must start with hunters demanding that their money be spent for its intended purpose and to actively engage their local elected officials to alter the manner in which these funds are being allocated. As a fisherman I have no problem including fish, stream, and pond restoration in this equation, as long as fishing gear is also taxed and as long as timber harvesting does not pollute or otherwise jeopardize the integrity of our clean waters. Only time will tell. Dealing with governments and particularly trying to change governance in these matters is never an easy task. It will take many hands to get it done, including all our politically active sportsman's organizations. But, get it done we must to insure the wise use of our natural resources and the wildlife that benefit from intelligent conservation practices. Sportsman must speak up now to have their tax dollars spent wisely for them.

Get Back Outdoors

Aside from the policy and political arena that we need to stay attuned to, the sporting public just wants to enjoy the outdoors and savor the hunt. Their license fees and donations will hopefully be used to protect the populations of critters they seek, while making connections with like-minded individuals and organizations. These human connections are the most essential and necessary. Most of us take for granted the ability to walk, climb and use our arms to carry, haul and check our balance on steep mountain terrain down to the lower valleys below. If we are healthy to pursue our passions, we are blessed. However, there are many disabled sportsman and veterans who still desire to go afield and get the chance to hunt. Fortunately there are a number of organizations that are helping the physically challenged to do just that. One that is close to my roots in New England is called 'Get Back Outdoors'. There are many obstacles that these sportsmen face trying to negotiate the tough terrain posed by rugged mountains and descending valleys. Thanks to Blaine Anthony and John Rackley's specially-designed wheelchair, disabled outdoorsmen have gained the ability to traverse uneven terrain with less effort. One major goal of the organization is to raise money to help produce more of these wheel chairs. Bingham Maine guide, Bob Howe, who operates Pine Grove Outfitters, has benefited from the Get Back Outdoors program. The wheelchairs have enabled him to guide handicapped veterans afield, so that they to, can enjoy the splendors of the great outdoors.

To help with their efforts and to learn more, see them on the web at
www.pinegroveprogram.com

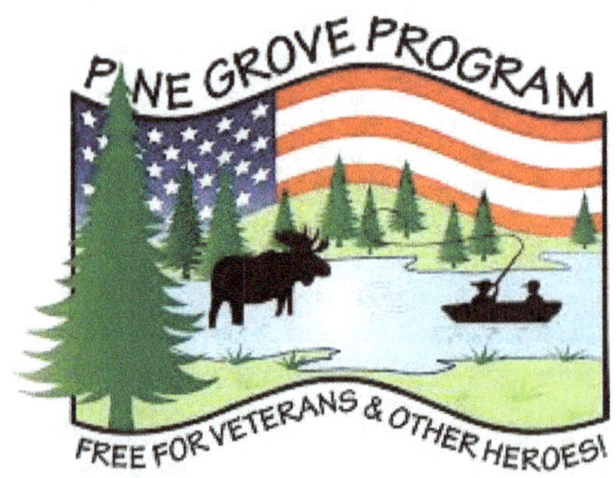

Chapter 9

Ed Nicholson & Teri Olson

Healing Waters

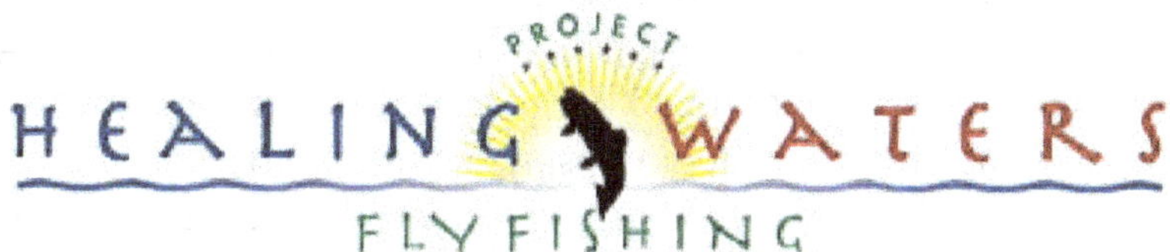

When sportsmen think of and use the five 'R's – recycle, restore, replace, renew and replenish, they are most often citing efforts to help with earth stewardship and the preservation of our fishing and hunting territories. As my nephew, Chris Johnson, reminded me the other day, true hunters and fisherman are the most active and best stewards of our lands and waters. They have a vested interest in keeping our waters and landscapes in their most 'natural' and productive state. They connect to these resources that have been handed down from one generation to the next to help keep family outdoor traditions alive. These connections are deeply rooted in the soil, rivers and lakes that span across this great country of ours. It is all about people joining together in common purposes and for the common good. These influences and traditions take on special significance when we engage those who need a helping hand or push in a better direction.

My first hands-on experience with Healing Waters was in the summer of 2010 at Aldro French's Forest Lodge located on the Rapid River in Maine. This location is remote and wild, but the trek in didn't discourage the dedicated fishing guides, partners and wide-eyed veterans. Members of the military drove or helicoptered in on that warm July afternoon to help and celebrate with the veterans as they casted their fly lines up and down the Rapid River. A hearty lunch and several comradely speeches to follow were in order. Aldro received a special award for his advanced efforts in promoting and hosting the day's events. Music was performed by Keith and Karin Jacobson, otherwise known as String Hackle. They performed their songs of Maine and country folk on the porch of the old Winter House overlooking the Lower Dam section of the river. Aldro is the owner of Forest Lodge and he, along with his companion Marie Johnston and the fishing guides he hires, take care of this historically significant property. This is where the famous author Louis Dickinson Rich wrote several of her best sellers, including her 1942 book, *We Took to the Woods*. Aldro and many others are dedicating their time to honor and rehabilitate our military people who need the outdoors, the sunshine, the river and the fish to lessen the pain, grief and heartache that they have been subjected to.

Project Healing Waters was founded in 2005 at the Walter Reed Medical Center by retired U.S. Navy Captain and avid fly fisherman Ed Nicholson. The germ of the idea behind this grass roots organization came to Ed after visiting and consoling war-torn soldiers and veterans who were suffering from physical and mental calamities. He recognized that many of these men and women had lost hope in life, were depressed and felt helpless in their dire circumstances. Ed knew that the fly fishing experience could bring much happiness, peace and tranquility to one's life and that these vets needed an outlet through this kind of out-of-doors encounter. His vision was to engage all of the nation's veteran hospitals with a program of getting the vets on the waters to fish with experienced angling guides. To get started, Ed got the attention of Teri Olson, recreation therapist at Maine's only veteran hospital in Togus, Maine. After hearing what Ed had to say, Teri went full throttle with the idea. As Teri told me, "Being a therapist and a fly fisher myself, I immediately recognized Ed's vision as a great one." Teri plugged Healing Waters programs into the hospital's schedule of necessary things to implement and progress with. Trout Unlimited members came and helped with teaching the vets how to fly cast, tie flies and to assist with at least one fishing trip each summer season. Teri networked with other hospitals around the country and the program grew rather quickly from state to state. Ed had emphasized that his goal was to help heal bodies, minds and souls through an ongoing program that worked directly with the hospital's transitioning agenda in such a way that lasting relationships would be born and nurtured. Today there are over 100 nationwide programs in 14 regions, including affiliates in Canada and England. Teri Olson has spent many decades helping the wounded to gain confidence and success in life. To this end she works with and supports many programs, but none work as well as Project Healing Waters. She states emphatically, "It is the only organization that does it totally correct. There's no politics involved, no second guessing. It's just people helping people and is geared to establishing long-term relationships that will last a lifetime. Friendships are made and friendships become everlasting." Teri continues: "The changes in the vets are magical to watch — breathtaking, very emotional and moving."

In contemplating Ed and Teri's definitions, purpose and networking successes, I reflect upon the reasons we fish and seek solace in the wilds of nature. Is it just the trophy fish we aspire to at the end of our lines, or is it something far more important than this self indulgence? We have at our disposal a wide variety of outdoor/fishing media and personalities that speak about the importance of conservation and preservation — the saving and restorations of rivers and native fish and game. As important as these missions are, do we lose sight of human connections and the inner dynamics of relationships that make life worth living? What compares to giving a helping hand to people whose lives teeter on the edge of life and death? Seeing people emerge into new personalities with a purpose for living within this shelter of grace and healing makes all our lives that much more meaningful and significant.

Ed, Teri and others saw the fruits of their labors when fishing guides and others gave of their time and energy to fish side by side with these soldiers who were freed from their four-walled, depressed-ridden hospital rooms. Many former sorrowful faces now had wide smiles and a reason for living and going forward. There was hope. There were people who cared. There was a reason to live. There was still beauty in this world to view, grasp and consume in wild, remote havens of clean waters and wild fish. They could now see the life of a river and the life that these waters gave back. Their focus changed from the worry of their wounds and their weary past to the quest of catching wild fish. The attention was now directed off of them and placed on the river's edge with a fly rod in hand. There was so much to learn—how to fly cast, reading the water, choosing the right fly, moving slow and easy and keeping alert to certain changes and challenges that always await the angler. To many, a whole new world had opened to them—a place to refresh, to find oneself, to repair and to restore that part of them that had been stolen or shaken from their inner beings. Yes, the peace, tranquility and magic that can only happen when confronted with flowing water at one's feet, the vista of jumping fish against the background of a yellow, sinking sun, the smell of sweet mist propelling over the rocks while gaining one's balance. The refreshed angler moves downstream and with every step more stability is gained, more confidence is acquired. As he leads his fish into the net he has gained his true freedom and possibly his first day of independence and happiness, as he revives the prize and releases it to live again.

"Give, and it will be given to you. A good measure, pressed down, shaken together and running over, will be poured into your lap.
For with the measure you use, it will be measured to you."

~ Luke: Chap. 6, Verse 3

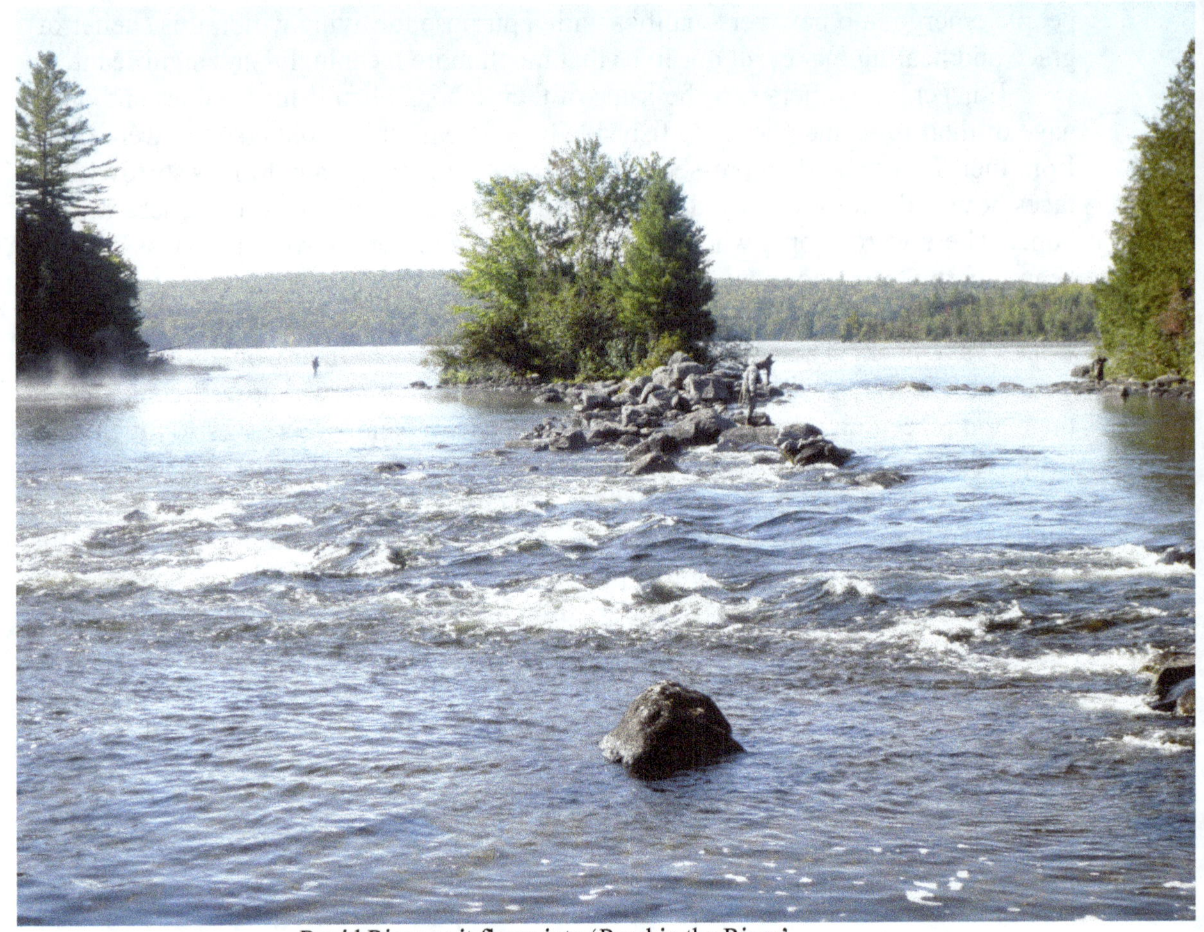

Rapid River as it flows into 'Pond in the River'

Chapter 10

Maine Trilogy

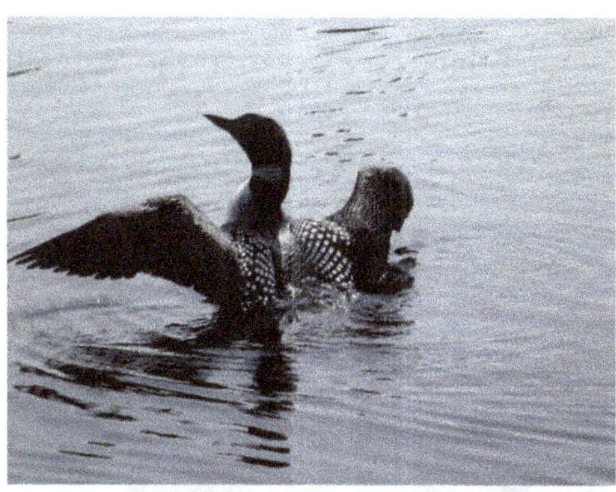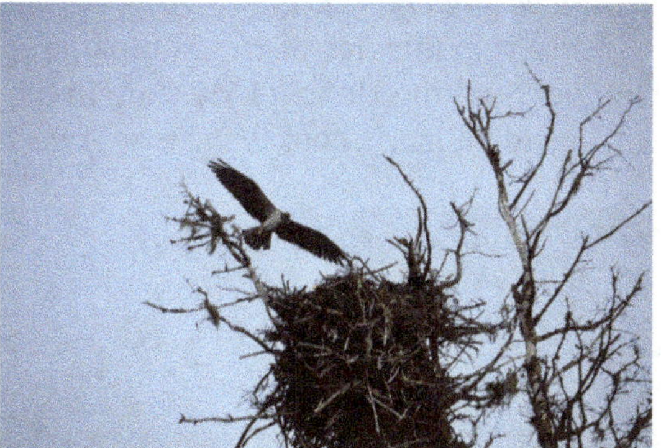

When one seeks to fly fish in the state that invented fly fishing in America, it's just a matter of locating the quadrant on the map that you want to pursue and go there. With eight or more distinct lake and river drainages and good angling results generated from each one, it can be a matter of scratching your head and biting your nails before deciding the ultimate direction. Personally, I'm often drawn to a deviating triangle that encompasses the geography of western Maine's Rangeley area up and over northeast to Moosehead Lake, with a final downeast drive to Washington County. It isn't just the great variety of rivers, lakes and ponds at one's disposal in these territories that appeals to me. I'm attracted to the history and nostalgia of each region and to the people there who have labored to preserve our fishing and hunting heritage.

The Rangeley and Oquossoc area harbors a number of pristine lakes that are connected directly via dams and rivers that hold good numbers of salmon and brook trout. Lakes of note include Rangeley, Kennebago, Mooselookmeguntic (Mooselook), Aziscohos, Cupsuptic, Upper and Lower Richardson and Umbagog. Between each of these lakes run rivers that have taken on the same name as the lake that gave them birth. A couple of notable brook trout and salmon rivers holding big, native fish that have not taken on their lake origin surnames are The Rapid and Magalloway Rivers.

Fly fishing in earnest began to flourish here in the late 1860s when the word got out that huge brook trout up to 8 lbs were being caught on a regular basis. People of note that paved the way and promoted the Rangeley sporting life included Cornelia "Fly Rod" Crosby, famed fly-tier Carrie Stevens, and the renaissance man of the

1940s and 50s, Herbie Welch. In Robert O.E. Elliot's 1950 book *All About Brook Trout*, he penned this superlative description of Mr. Welch's fly casting: *"In the graceful, rhythmic motions, the natural beauty of his casting style, there is artistry, giving expression to those nuances of longing, emotion and poetry that lie dormant in all true angler's hearts."*

To soak in this rich history, I highly recommend that travelers visit the Rangeley Outdoor Sporting Heritage Museum in the town of Oquossoc and read R. Donald Palmer's book *Images of America — Rangeley Lakes Region*.

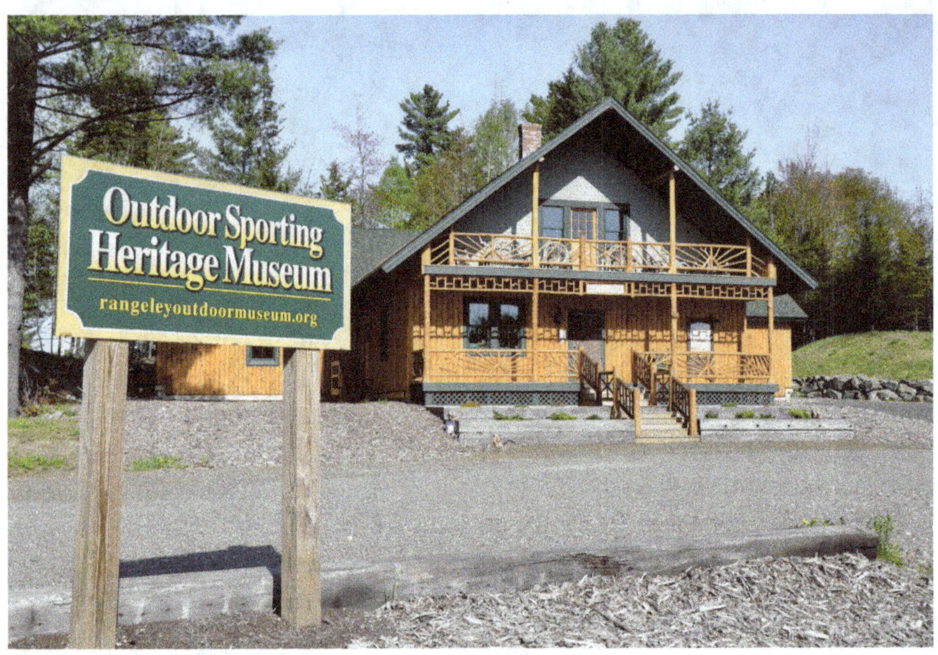

The best river fishing opportunities for large, native brookies and salmon are where these rivers are connected to lakes. Most often the finest time to wet your line in these waters is mid-May through late June, and again in late August through the end of September, after which many of these rivers become closed to fishing. Cold-flowing waters and spawning urges are primarily responsible for generating the ultimate fishing experience. For large brook trout up to 6 lbs, the Rapid River is one of my favorite destinations. Anglers can access this remote stream from the 14-mile long Fish Pond Road off Route 16 or from Lower Richardson Lake via boat. Camping sites are dotted here and there along the lake. For more comfortable arrangements, the historic 1853 Lakewood Camps or Forest Lodge beckon you. Both camps have seasoned guides to help navigate the river with tried and true fly patterns. Kris Thompson, who operates Pond In The River Guide Service in Rangeley, has much experience and know how in this area and comes highly recommended. The Rapid begins its flow at the Lower Richardson's Lake outlet at Middle Dam and cascades swiftly down to the 'Pond In The River'. The flow out of the pond runs wide and smooth to Lower Dam, after which it picks up speed on its 'rapid' descent to Umbagog Lake.

There are hundreds of spectacular pools and rock-pockets that allow for easy fly-casting along the whole waterway. Whether you prefer nymphing, streamers, wets or dry-flies, the river equally accommodates all techniques. For any rivers beginning their descents at dams, it is important to check on the water flow before planning a trip. Spring run offs can be high and, if so, many rivers including the Rapid become unfishable. Usually water flows measured in cubic feet per second (cfs) that fall under 1500 are acceptable. This spring I netted a few hefty 3 to 5 lb brookies and salmon up to 3 lbs on size 16 to 18 dark and light Hendrickson dries. Often, however, the conditions are such that nymphing with the help of an indicator float is the only reliable method of extracting large brookies from their deep rocky lairs. All of the local rivers have diverse aquatic life and dependable hatches, and it is always wise to carry a good variety of fly patterns. There are over 375 mayfly species in Maine alone, and even with a fly shop strapped to your back, you might not have what the fish are after. The tried and true Adams dry in various colors and sizes is a must for any angler's fly box, as well as brown, red and green caddis wets to bump along the bottom.

Rapid Hatch Fever

A couple months prior to a 'Healing Waters' event that my family took part in on the Rapid River, I was fishing with my daughter Karin along the Lower Dam section. We both caught a few solid trout in several of these wide-spread classic pools, but nothing was coming easy and the big boys weren't obliging. I moved down and began fishing several holding pools off Lower Dam's wooden remains, while Karin was doing the same on several slot openings to my right. Karin noticed several large brookies rising for flies just at the edge of the dam's wooden underpinnings where fast-flowing water entered the pool. She tied on a size 16 dark grey bodied mayfly dry. Her moment of sheer concentration began by dimpling the fly softly just above and to the side of her and letting it glide over the feeding trout. After a few casts, her rod bent over with a vicious take as her voice rose to alert me to the noise of the line zinging off the reel. "Keep its head up!" I repeatedly yelled to her over the noise of the river's surge. The pounding of her rod and the size of the swirling tail crashing the surface was all the evidence I needed to know that this was a nice fish. "I'm comin' Karin! I'll get to the back of the eddy and net 'em for ya. Just keep good pressure on. Wear 'em out. Keep the head up out of those sharp bottom rocks!" With my typical fatherly overreaction, I must have repeated myself several times.

Finally, climbing gingerly down into the rocks with my outreached hand, Karin held
tight and eased the 4 lb trout into the net. We balanced the brightly-colored brookie
in the water, snapped a quick photo and gently released her back into the depths.
Karin is a very skilled and savvy fly-fisher who can handle any given challenge. She
certainly didn't need any of my guidance, but I know she appreciated my
enthusiasm. I was glad I didn't goof things up.

Her morning wasn't finished. Soon after, another similarly-sized trout on the
same dry fly came to net. Only this time as we peered into the net there was another
small green fly tucked into the fish's cheek. Plucking it off she exclaimed, "This is
Keith's fly! This is Keith's special Pilgrim Caddis fly!" We both laughed in unison.
Karin's husband Keith told us that he had gotten broken off in the rocks by a large
brookie the day before. "Well Karin," I said gesturing with a blink in my eye,
"You're going to have to give your husband a lesson on how to keep the head up on
these big brookies."

"Ya dad, your right," she said, and again we broke out in a hearty laugh. What a
joy it was spending time with my daughter at such a dynamic moment as this. Being
able to share some of these great wonders of the world with your kids makes these
experiences just that much more special and gratifying.

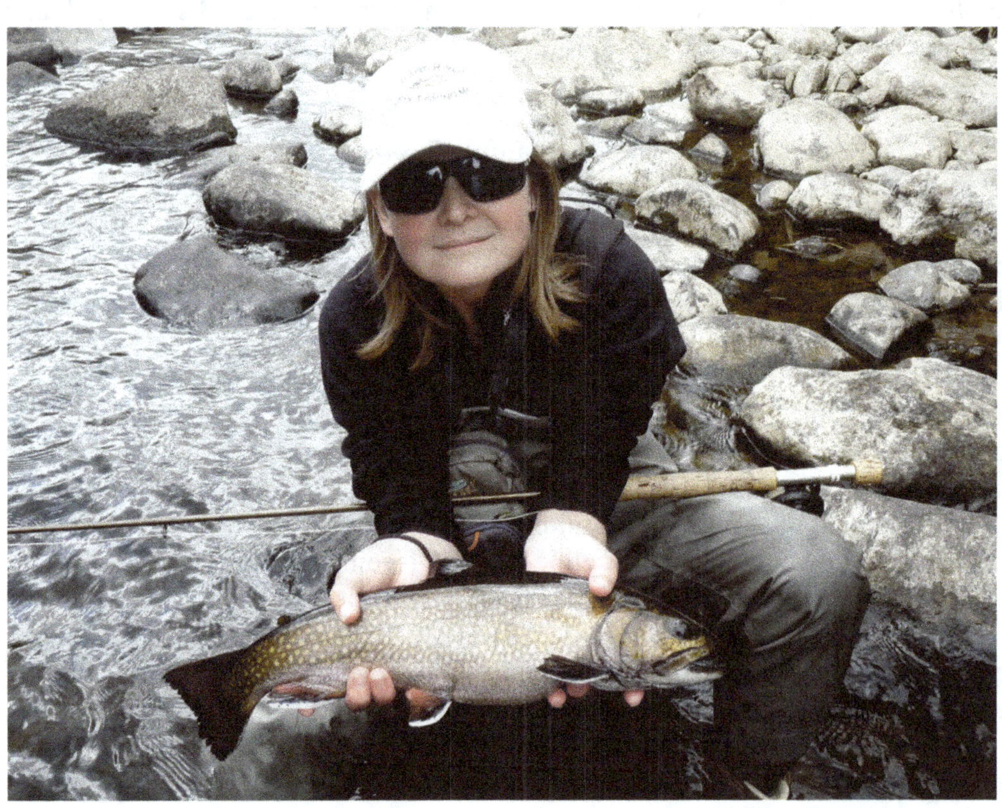

After several more hookups with trout and leaping salmon we headed over to visit our friends Aldro French and his partner and dutiful assistant Marie Johnston at Forest Lodge's Winter House. They prepared a nice lunch for us on the front porch overlooking one the most picturesque views of this beautifully landscaped river. After chewing the fat for an hour or so and catching up on each other's lives, we bid adieu and biked our way back up the rugged trail to the car. Arriving at the cabin in the town of Oquossoc we showed Keith the fly that we had salvaged from his lost fish. "You gotta be kiddin me! Ya, that's my fly!" was his reply as his eyes lit up. Fish stories big and small around the campfire that evening consumed our conversation. Keith retired his fly to a prominent old piece of driftwood hanging over the edge of the cabin's cupboard.

The Kennebago River gets its start from the upper Kennebago Lakes. The best access point is from Grant's Camps Lodge and Cabins located on the lake. As is the case with most of Maine's remote camps, this one is again filled with history and nostalgia. The river's lower reaches can be accessed by car and hiking, with the option of biking upstream along an old train steam engine bed. I enjoy taking along a lunch for a day trip and reaching some of the prime upper waters on my bike. For the most part, this river fishes good year round with its abundant water flow emptying 12 miles from its source into Cupsuptic Lake, which, in turn, is attached to the larger Mooselook Lake. My quest is to catch larger salmon and trout that have come up from the lake, and on occasion 3 to 5 lb salmon and brook trout are obliging. Viewing moose, deer and partridge (ruffed grouse) are all in a day's work when prodding along these riverbanks steeped in deep woods, beauty and preservation. On my last visit this past June I managed to net several leaping salmon up river on Black Ghost and Gray Ghost streamers — both famous flies originated in the area by historic locals Herbie Welch and Carrie Stevens.

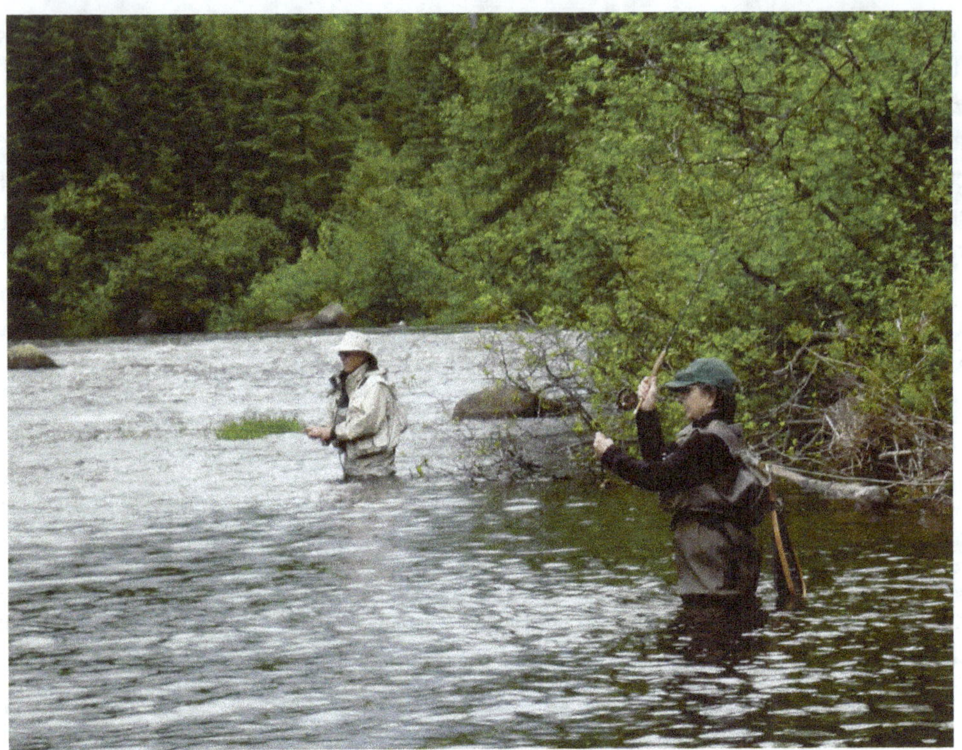

John and Liz Bacon trying to forge high water on a raging Kennebago River

Traveling in the northeast direction to the Moosehead Lake region takes about 3 hours of leisurely driving time. Upon arriving at the southern tip of the lake in Greenville, my first stop is Dan Legere's Maine Guide Fly Shop to peruse over the fly selections, pick up a few more leaders and find out about the fishing conditions. From Greenville north on either side of the lake, one could get lost on hundreds of meandering lumbering roads that take you to prime trout and salmon waters. It would take several lifetimes to even touch a portion of this vast territory with its lengthening arms stretching up into the remote Allagash region. Delorme's *The Maine Atlas and Gazetteer* is always at my side to help navigate through this wild countryside. The west and east outlets of the Kennebec River and the Moose River are accessed by driving up on the west side of Moosehead Lake. Float trips can be arranged on the Kennebec, which has excellent fly fishing for salmon, rainbows and brook trout. The smaller Moose River is best fished in late spring or fall. When the water flow conditions are right, the fish are cooperative. Spotted here and there are many ponds that have healthy populations of brook trout. There is something magic about boating out and casting to rising trout just as the red sun begins to set at the end of the day. The beauty, peace and serenity realized quickly reminds me again of what's important in life, and why it is a priority to take the time to soak in the magnificent splendors that the earth filters through our senses.

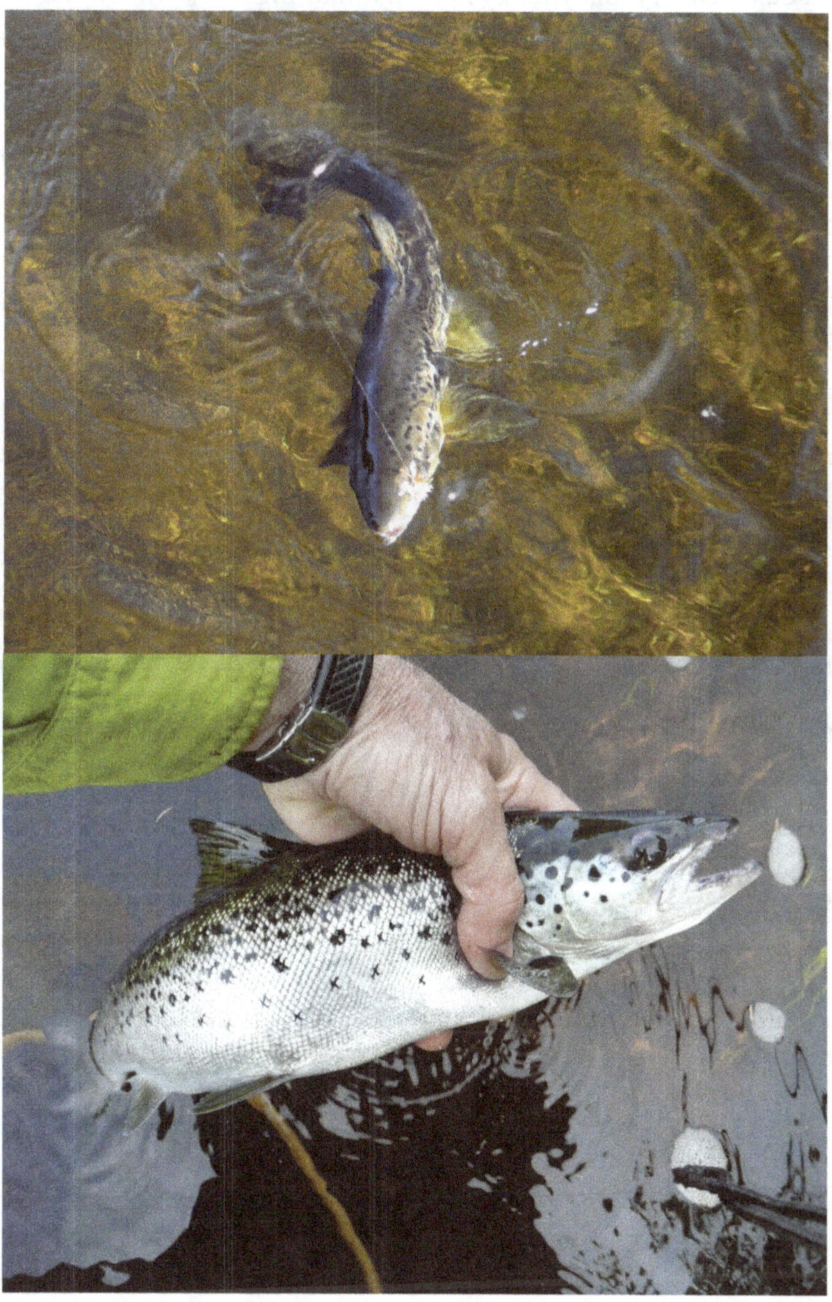

A favorite fall destination prior to heading up the West Branch of the Penobscot River and beyond is the Roach River, located in Kokadjo on the eastern side of Moosehead Lake. Don't blink your eyes when motoring into town or you may miss it. The approaching sign says "Welcome to Kokadjo — Population: Not Many."

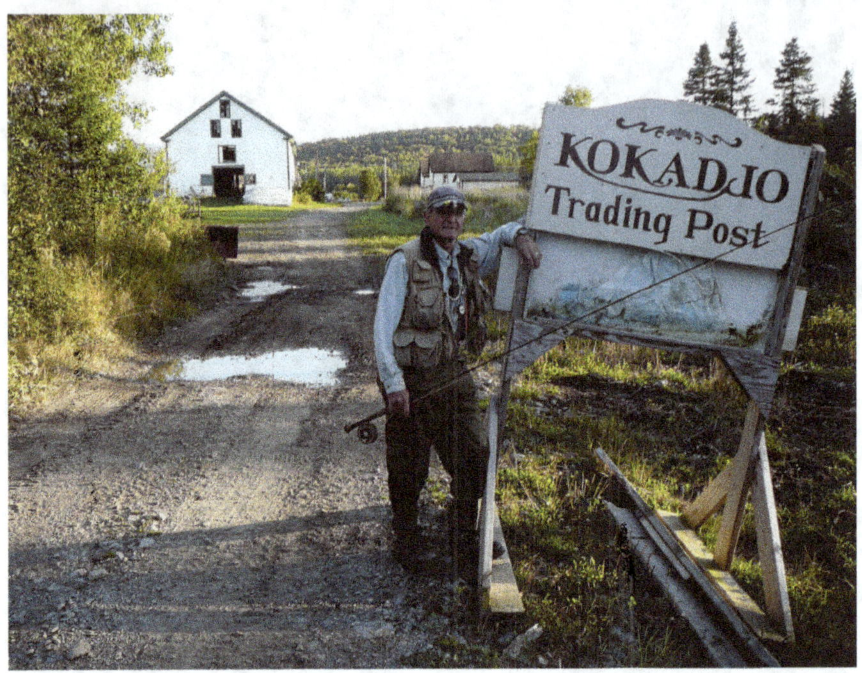

The Roach begins at First Roach Pond and meanders several miles before emptying into the lake. It typifies what many wading fly fisherman prefer with its mid-size width, graveled strewn riffles, long runs and deep pools. Spawning salmon and trout can be found the entire length of the river with many tough-to-get-to pools holding 'fresh fish' that have just navigated up from the lake. Needless to say, the action can be fast and furious with a mix of good-sized lake-grown salmon and brook trout. The Roach is only one of a few major rivers in Maine that is designated as a 'fly-fishing only', and 'catch and release' fishery. The state has purchased much of the land adjacent to the river as a buffer against any development due to the river's importance as a spawning ground and nursery. Some of the most tantalizing and heart-stopping pools include Dump, Corner, Warden's, Spring and Slaughter. Last fall I hiked in to explore over a mile of river, and at every likely holding place, I netted several salmon and/or trout. As I was casting the Dave Footer Special diagonally across the river and retrieving the line with quick, pumping strokes, a 4 lb salmon took the streamer on the upswing and proceeded to immediately go airborne and dance repeatedly along the back of the pool. The strength of the fish against the current repeatedly sent my line zinging off the reel. For ten minutes I held on and managed to wheedle the fish into calmer water for a quick photo and release. This picture was played out numerous times on that pleasant fall day with some riffles and pools producing over six or more large brookies and salmon. I reached into my memory bank trying to recall such an exhilarating angling moment as this. I couldn't think of one. Comfortable cabin lodging and boat rentals on Roach Pond are available at the Trading Post Store operated by Fred and Marie Candeloro. There is also excellent fishing for lake trout, salmon and brookies in all of the three Roach Ponds that are connected to each other via connecting streams.

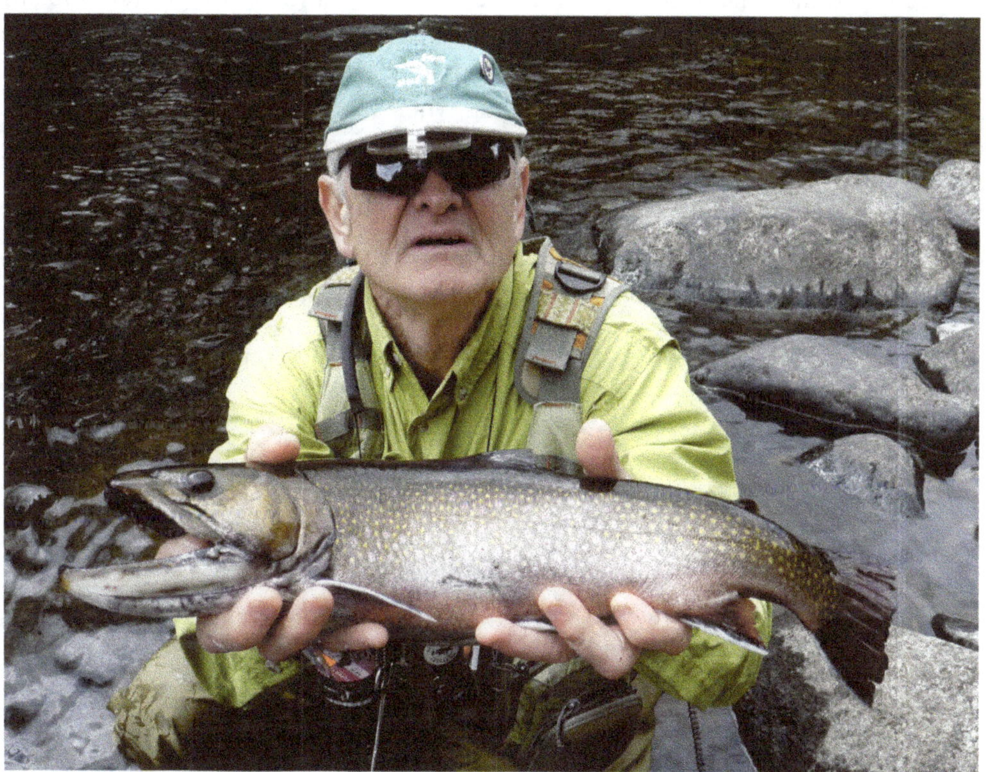

From the Moosehead region we travel southeast to the smallmouth bass fishing capital of the Northeast. Washington County holds some of Maine's largest lakes, with a plethora of beautiful ponds and fabulous rivers. Along the coast in this 'Down East' sector many once famous sea-run salmon rivers empty into the ocean north of Acadia National Park. These include the Dennys, Machias and Narraguagus rivers. As a kid I remember my dad coming home from his Maine fishing excursions with hefty salmon from Spednik and West Grand Lakes. When I first fished this area over

40 years ago, we experienced fantastic fly fishing for smallmouth bass in Baskahegn Lake. As the local corner store market owner remarked before venturing there to try our luck, "Boys, they don't call it Baskahegan fer nothing! Aye yup!" Those memories made many years ago rekindle my desire to return today to Grand Lake Stream. This short 5 mile river runs out of West Grand Lake and empties into Big Lake. If your number one goal is to catch a good number of salmon on just about any fly you put on the end of your leader, then this is the place for you. Best time to fish here typically is between early May through mid-June and then again in the Fall. I've caught fish on hendricksons, caddis flies, nymphs, streamers, woolybuggers (leech patterns) and dry flies. If you prefer lake fishing, trout, salmon and bass are plentiful in both lakes. In the village of Grand Lake Stream one can catch up on the news and fishing action at the Pine Tree General Store as well as at many lodges and inns that dot the landscape. World class Weatherby's Lodge is at the rivers edge and the area has an abundance of seasoned guides who can hone you in on the best waters.

I always count each day a special blessing when I venture into the Maine woods to test my mettle with my two most favorite fish — brook trout and salmon. Enjoy the Maine outdoor experience. For sure, it's like no other.

"Sweet, sweet surrender. Live, live without care.
Like the fish in the water, like the bird in the air"

~John Denver

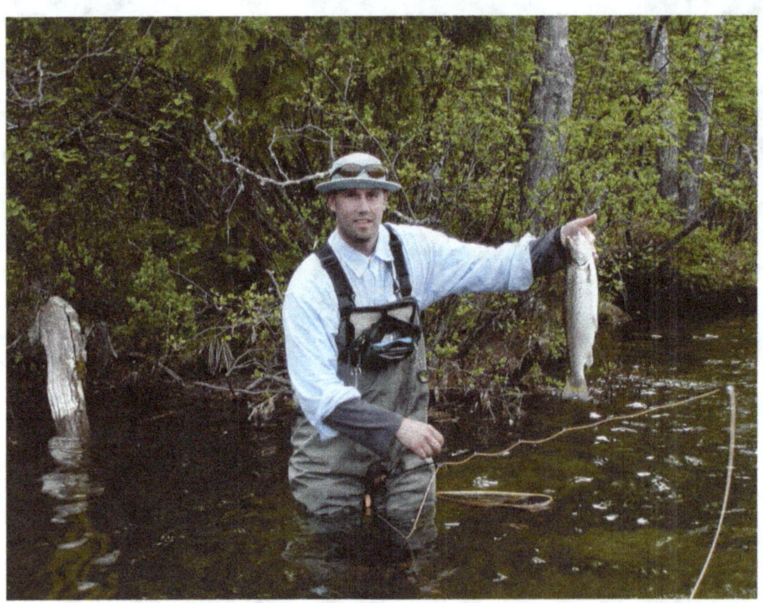

Karin's husband Keith with nice Grand Lake Stream salmon

Lure

    for Dad

The air always smelled of bug spray and spruce
When our voices trailed to whispers, rigging up our rods,
Feet scuffling over gravel at the back hatch
Where you'd tie a wet fly on my neophyte line.

Words like "monofilament" and "Grey Ghost" buzzed
As I lumbered into oversized waders.
I, a curious student of the earth, my pages budding,
Following the sure-footed towards distant rushing,
Down leafy slopes of dry oak and birch, spring's branches
Waving shadows like ripples on the water.

The ground leveled and moistened, fiddleheads hugged
A nameless brook. You snapped some from their stocks
For dinner and ripped sheet moss off a rock for our creels
To keep our coming query cool.

Our steps slackened and the shaded river was a presence
Like some other gravity, a crashing well of safely-kept secrets
Only divulged in pieces, never fully, to a patient and quiet listener
Fully in tune with the liquid symphony.

I watched you read the swirling pool,
The circling question marks you waded into
And cast a slack line into mystery;
Then rake a muddler minnow past a boulder midstream
until white flashing resistance —
Your rod and arm lifted swiftly in a single arc
And you snickering shyly at your luck
At the sure strike deep and layered like currents of perception.

It was dusk when we found the truck and headed home
With our creels half full and bottomless,
And my heart with a barbed hook in it
Always pulling me back.

Karin Johnson – Editor, Teacher, Poet, Songwriter/Musician

Author's daughter

Chapter 11

Quebec Rendezvous

Northern Quebec's Caniapiscau River caught my fancy a few years ago and several of my pals were eager to get back to this remote area almost 900 miles north of our Massachusett homes. The Beaver float plane journey 100 miles northwest of Wabush/Labrador City enhanced our anticipation on this blue-sky day. The horizon was dotted with low-hanging puffy cumulus clouds flushed against a white lichen terrain spiked with thick clusters of spruce and interloping waterways. Our eyes were here to search for and to test our fly-fishing mettle against some of North America's largest and most tenacious salmon, brook trout and pike. Jumping with teenage enthusiasm off the plane, we were greeted by our guides Bertin, Michael, Clyd and Norman. Bertin Gagne has been the head guide for Club Chambeaux for 16 years. Michael and Norman are native Indians from the Montagnais tribe located above Quebec City near Lake St. John. Along with Clyd, they are highly experienced with fishing and hunting in this vast wilderness territory. Four of us including Dave Fox, Phil Ethier and Terry McGovern, had been here before. Maine resident newcomers with high hopes were my cousin Barry Lundquist and Jeff Armstrong. For anglers seeking other adventures from the Wabush mining town junction, the McKenzie River Lodge is also a prize location for similar fishing experiences, with a location of 125 miles to the northeast.

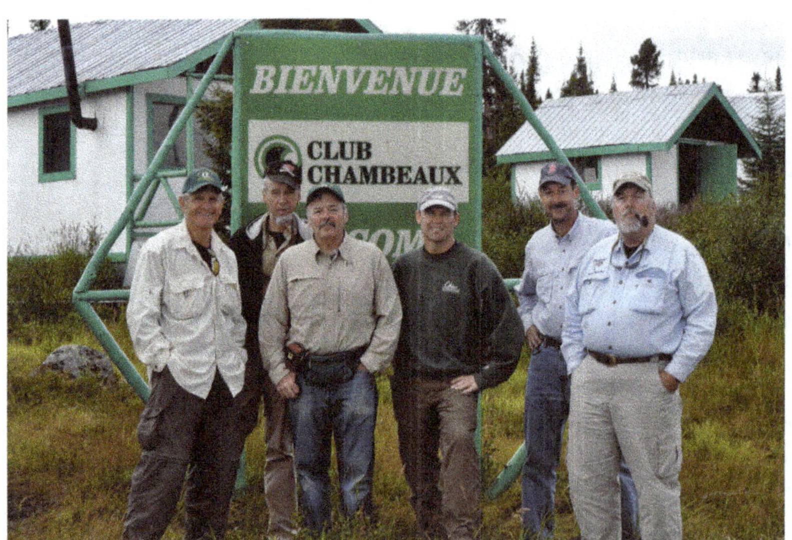

Tom, Jeff, Terry, Phil, Barry, Dave (our fly tying expert)

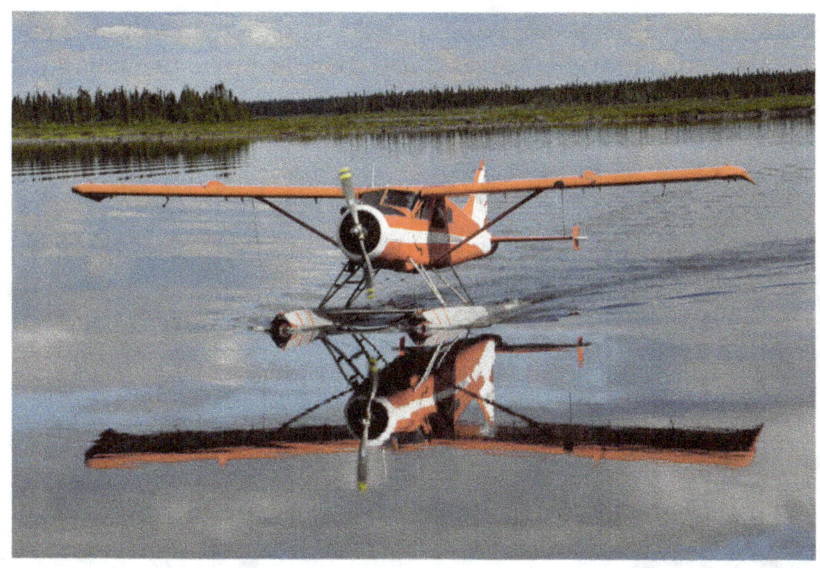

The Caniapiscau Reservoir is the second largest reservoir in Canada covering over 14,000 square miles. Our Camp #1 is located about 50 miles from this main body of water which helps to produce some of Quebec's largest salmon (Quananiche). This location is in northern Quebec's 'discontinuous permafrost' zone where the land is vegetated by boreal forest that can only be reached by float planes. Because of this inaccessibility, there are thousands of square miles of wilderness habitat safety for large brook trout, salmon and indigenous animals such as black bear, woodland caribou, moose, mink and otter.

In late summer and fall the salmon feel the urge to spawn and leave the lake to journey up the river. The watercourse is generally wide and rocky, with outlying thinner waters mixed in the midst of rocks and islands. There are many miles of deep pools, rocky falls and smooth runs. The fast flowing water is very diverse and most often challenging to the fly fishing angler. The rivers main course, particularly in our location and to the southwest of us, often breaks up into narrower flows, which makes for dramatic wading experiences for brookies and salmon. This river diversity gives much variety to our fly fishing experience, and this feeling of casting into new and distant waters each day added measurably to our adventure. In these faster running flows are found good numbers of brightly colored brook trout that are attracted to most any fly presented to them. We had good luck tying on brown, green and white bomber dries and running them through the rapids and edges of pools and rocks. One 4 lb male brookie smashed the bomber as it sped to the end of one of these runs, and immediately torpedoed airborne. "Bert," I acclaimed, "this trout thinks it's a salmon! Awesome!" The trout would 'keep house' just above and up from the slower lower pool-emptying waters where pike predators were waiting to ambush anything that moved. Several large trout had pike teeth markings on their sides or were missing part of their tails due to pike encounters.

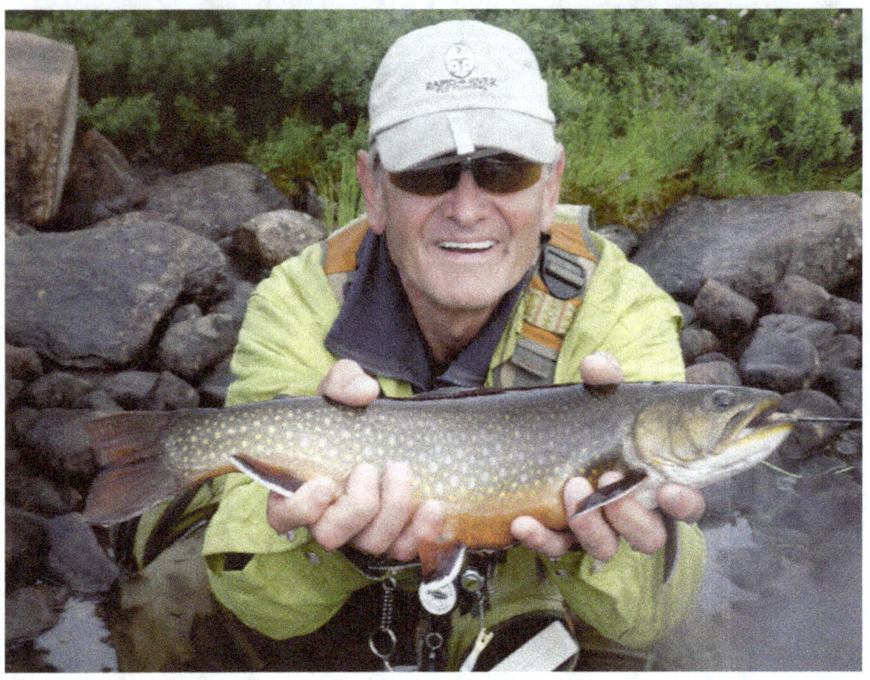

　　We would start each day with a sumptuous breakfast served by master chef Liliane Bergeron. Then we would hook up with our guides and boat to various destinations. First we would troll for salmon and then stop here and there to wade and cast. Later in the morning we motored into a mix of salmon and trout waters prior to a waterside lunch. I set up two rods for each day's excursion. The 8-weight Orvis Hydros rod was used for trolling with a sink-tip line to keep the fly down in the strike zone. The river currents are very swift and powerful and without a sinking line the streamer flies would just dimple along the top crest of the water. Although hungry salmon and trout would still likely take the trolled fly as it bumped and splashed over the surface, I found more good fortune when it plied its way just under the waters crest. The accompanying lighter 6-weight Thomas & Thomas was used when I would sturdy myself against the currents while wading and casting into likely holding pools and eddies. Both rods have stiffer 'fast actions' to assist with longer casts in windy conditions and to help budge large fish against the river's fast-flowing currents and rocky bottoms. When trolling, I used tandem streamers that hopefully would attract larger fish. Most any pattern worked well, including Mickey Finns, Black and Grey Ghosts, Magog Smelts and Dave Footer Specials. Since the landlocks here have been caught in the 20 lb range with sharp, razor cutting teeth, a minimum 10 to 12 lb leader is most advisable.

One afternoon just prior to our shore lunch at 'The Falls' below Camp 1, Bert maneuvered the boat along the back of a wide pool when my rod suddenly bent over with a thunderous hit and the scream of my line zipping off the reel. "Bert, this is a mighty fish!" The fish only took one giant leap out of the water and we surmised that it must be a female full of eggs to warrant such low profile behavior. The fight carried on for over 35 minutes with many powerful runs and rod-bending action. Even when the finned monster decided not to make any more dramatic runs, I failed to move it off the river's bottom. Bert peered into the water as I got the fish close to the boat on several tries. He thought that because of its size it must be a lake trout. "No Bert, I saw silver on this fish, and I know it's a mighty *salmo salar*." Finally, we slowly maneuvered the boat into calmer water and I pulled tight and led the fish into Bert's net. Yes, a large female salmon indeed. I breathed deeply with a sigh of relief. Bert's sturdy, rugged face turned into a wide smile. "Wow, what a fish!" I exclaimed. We kept the fish wet in the net over the side of the boat while I frantically pried my camera out for a couple quick photos before reviving and releasing this superior Caniapiscau River specimen back into the waters. We didn't weigh or measure the fish since we didn't want to further risk its life after such a long extended tussle, but we estimated the weight at about 15 lbs. Certainly the largest landlocked salmon I ever caught and it was the largest salmon netted by Bert that summer of 2011. Most of the salmon we caught were in the 5 to 10 lb range.

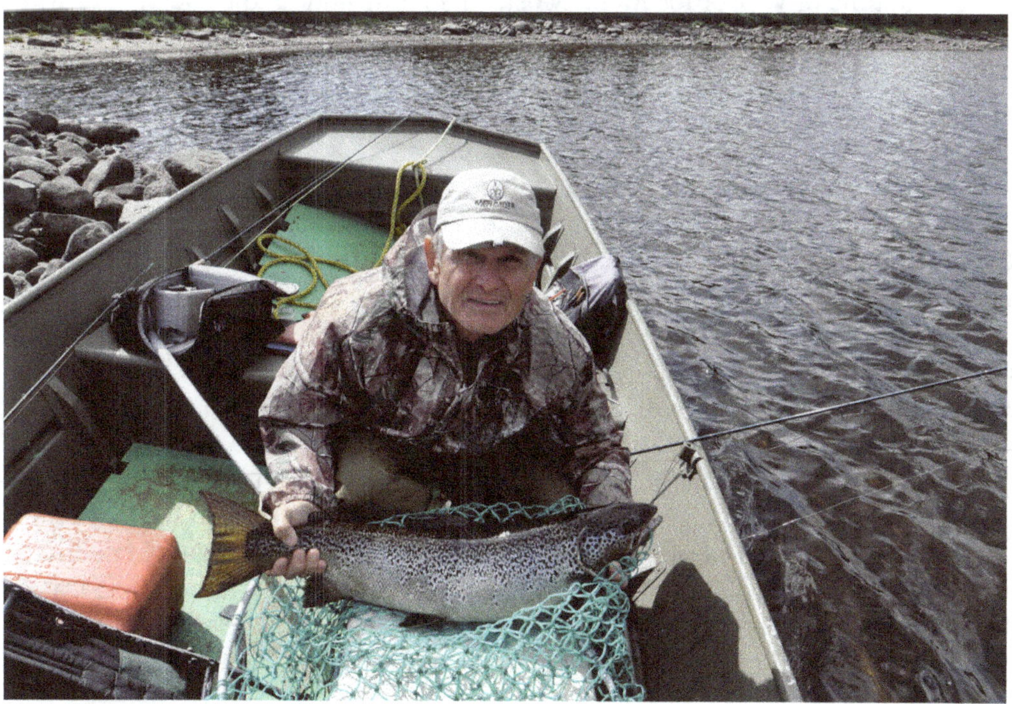

I have fished numerous times for sea-run Atlantic salmon in New Brunswick, Quebec and Nova Scotia. These fish are often larger than their landlocked cousins due to the ocean's abundant food sources and nutrients, but, pound for pound, they fight no harder than these landlocks. In fact landlocks sometimes fight harder. When encountering a 'fresh' sea-run salmon, their tenacity, fight and leaping flights are in the x-zone. However, if these salmon have been in the river for several weeks or months, their stamina, strength and determination has been compromised by their long endurance test against the river's currents, lack of eating, and their instinctive requirement to save energy for propagating the species. It is no wonder that their energies become depleted after a 10 to 50 mile run up against a river's current and cascading falls. With persistent and patient fly casting, the angler may entice these fish to take an offering. Once hooked, the salmon may not leap or go on too many dynamic tail outs. Often, fish in this condition seek the bottom of pools and sulk there, and even when added rod pressure is applied in an attempt to pry them out of the depths, it is often difficult to move them.   This is particularly true of females (hens) who are heavy with eggs, and this behavior may be attributed to their innate need to conserve energy. A quick catch, recovery and release is imperative when handling these warriors of the river in order to give them the best chance of survival. In comparison, I've never met a landlocked salmon that didn't fight tenaciously, no matter what time of year or location. Most, smaller in stature to be sure, but true leaping fighters and line-stretchers to the end. To dispel any argument, all wild salmon are members of the 'royal family'—all are equal in my world of study and quest for them.

While Bert and Clyde were preparing lunch under an uphill tent platform that had been recently shaken apart by a black bear looking for leftovers, Jeff, Barry and I waded cautiously out along rocky outreaches, casting to likely holding lairs for trout and salmon. Some of the lee water held giant pike and we caught a few to mix with the river side lunch each day. I had tied on a brook trout streamer and on the second cast there was a quick bump and the fly was gone — surely a pike had managed to get its teeth into the leader. So I avoided this stretch and kept the next streamer fly in the currents plying around the rocky outcroppings. I managed to catch a couple 2-lb trout while Barry and Jeff fared better with nice salmon and bigger trout. With hunger pangs and the smell of the fire permeating my lungs, I began the trek off of the slippery rocks and almost made it to shore before slipping and going headfirst into the brisk water. Holding my fly rod high to avoid breaking it and using my left arm as a lever, I didn't stay submerged for too long — just long enough to cool myself down and feel the dribbles of wetness working its way down my boots. With a definite tone of amusement in their voices, the guys yelled, "Hey, how's the swimming? There's no lifeguard on duty. Are you all right?"

"Ya, A-OK, but I think I'm half left! Ha! Ya haven't really fished hard unless ya take a dip now and then." This was a reminder to always keep the wader belt tied tightly around the waist just in case these slips happen in deeper water. With minimal insect activity due to the cool winds, I was able to strip down to the waist and let the clothes dry in the afternoon sun. Lunch, as usual, was scrumptious with a mix of fried shake-n-bake fish chunks, salad, corn, beans and Liliane's delicious cookies for dessert.

Dave, Phil and Terry were generally off fishing in some opposite direction from us. Above Chambeaux Falls they had good luck with large salmon — the largest weighing 9 lbs that Dave snaked on a Grey Ghost streamer. Latter in the week at the same location, Jeff netted a 12 pounder while Barry leapfrogged with a 10 pounder. In the mix with these powerful swimmers were numerous 4 to 5 lb salmon and 2 to 5 lb brook trout. Phil and Terry had a blast with trout banging their dry fly presentations with regularity. Although there is some insect activity, there is no need in these climes to 'match the hatch' as is often the case back in the States. As the summer proceeds and gets closer to the fall, these fish are hungry and are ready to eat most anything going by their radar zone.

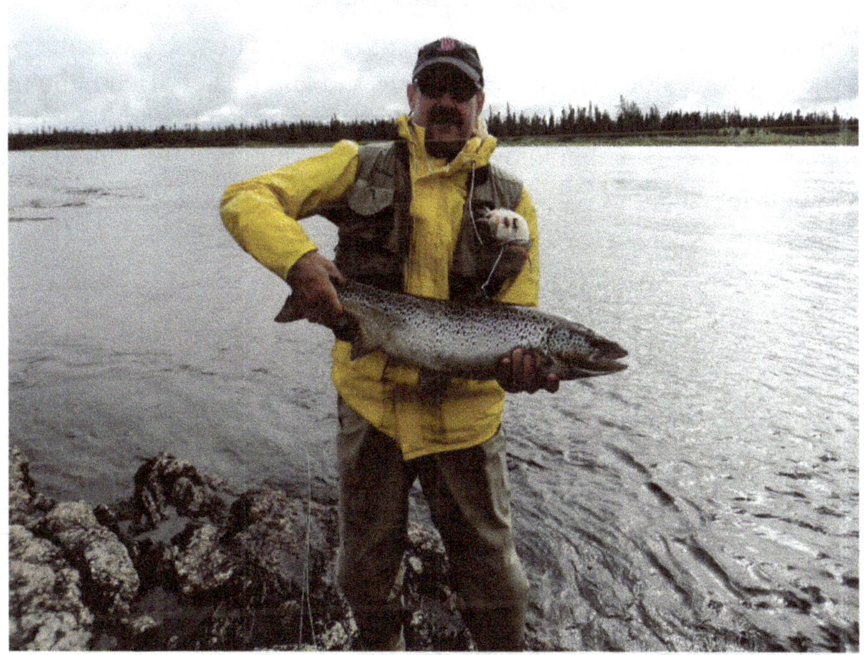

Barry with hefty line-zipping salmon

One of the highlights of the trip and an episode that brought much laughter and buoyant conversation was the news that Jeff had netted a 20-lb lake trout after an hour's battle. Prior to our trip, Jeff had expressed the disappointment he had on a jaunt he took to the deep woods a few years ago. The outfitter advertised the big brookies and salmon commonly caught, but Jeff only managed to pull in one laker after another while being eaten alive by hoards of blood-sucking black flies. It was what Jeff referred to kindly as "A miserable trip from hell." He continued with, "Those damn lakers — I swore that I never wanted to catch another one of those slimy, grotesque trout again." However, since this particular bottom dwelling trout was caught on a 7 weight G-Loomis fly rod borrowed from Barry with an affixed tandem orange-red streamer that I rented to Jeff, and given that it was the only laker caught on the trip, Jeff seemed quite pleased. He was further amused and enthused to learn from Clyd that it was the largest laker taken on a fly in the river that the guide could remember in his fifteen years of service to Camp Chambeaux. It was more likely to encounter this trout species in the late spring when the river waters are as cold as the lake where these fish migrate from. Catching one in the river in August was unusual and we all agreed, special — particularly due to the size and feisty fight of this giant.   However, to keep up our jovial humored spirits, we didn't let Jeff forget for the remainder of the trip that lakers must have an affection and definite attraction to him, and that he was the king of these slimy and smelly trout bottom dwellers. Sadly in January, 2016 Jeff Armstrong passed away from complications of cancer. Visiting with him shortly before his passing, his wish was to live on, to venture to other fishing and hunting destinations. He was the owner of Jeff's Marine in Thomaston, Maine. He was a solid and trusted friend, the man I bought my Parker boat from and the man who introduced me to some good fishing and hunting territories. The man known as the 'boat king' and the 'pirate of the waters' will long be remembered in the annals of Maine coastal lore.

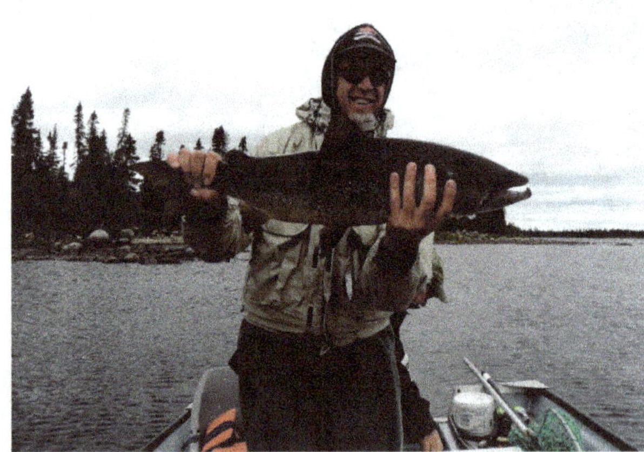

Jeff happy with large salmon

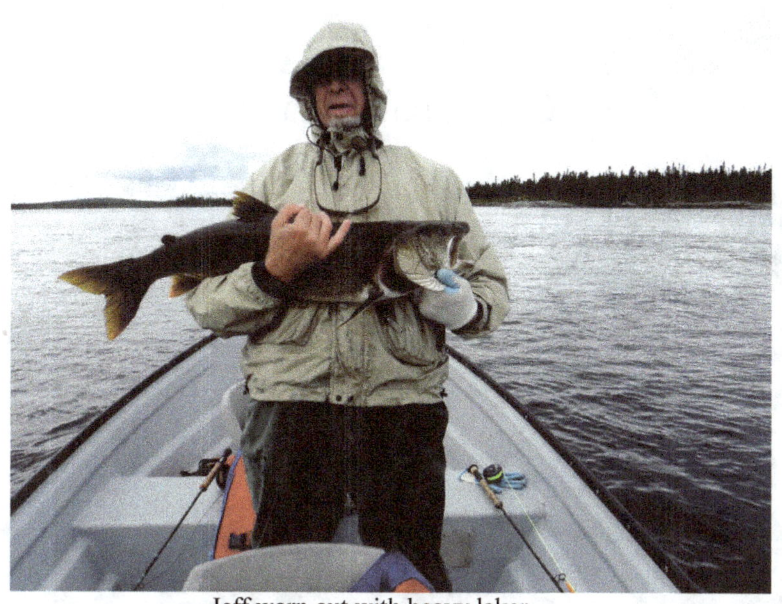

Jeff worn out with heavy laker

The weather held up well except for one late afternoon hour when black, thunderous clouds rolled in. With lighting strikes cascading on the horizon, the skies let loose with a torrential downpour of rain mixed with cannonball hailstones. Hurriedly we reeled in our lines and sped a quick retreat back to the camp. When the hammering downpours finally ceased, the sun-setting sky became a magnificence of orange, red, white and blues that reflected off the water. Everyone grabbed their cameras to capture the painted distant horizon that bled with nature's wonder. What a special place this is. What an extraordinary treat to share it with friends.

"We love to expect, and when expectation is either disappointed or gratified, we want to be again expecting."

~Samuel Johnson

Cape Breton Magic

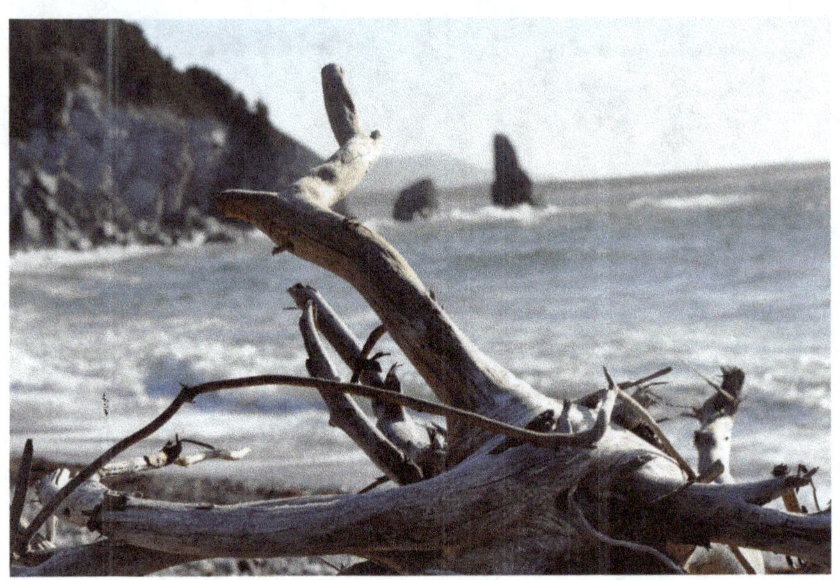

For a number of years I have been itching to return to Nova Scotia's magnificent Margaree Valley and its famed Margaree River. My new fly-fisher wife Pam was equally looking forward to the fishing, combined with touring the majestic Cabot Trail. We dovetailed our journey so that it coincided with the 'Celtic Colours' week in October and the annual Margaree Salmon Association's dinner/auction fundraiser. Celtic Colour's venues take place in over 30 picturesque Cape Breton Island communities, where some of the world's best musicians spin their talents with fiddle, guitar and piano. Scottish music mixed with a tinge of French and Irish influence in some locals is certainly entwined within the heart and soul of these rural villages. Many of the compositions, both from new and historic origin, speak to the hardships, the faith, the hope and durability of a people who have endured by using the earth and sea's resources as their sustenance for many generations.

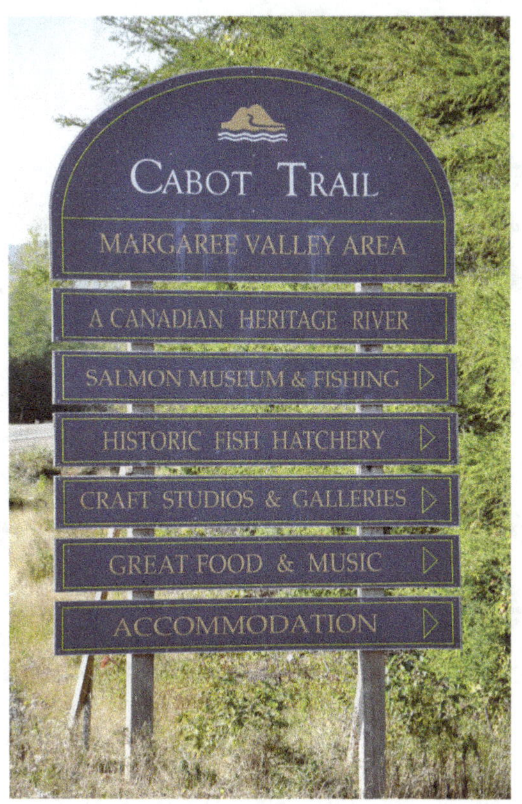

CABOT TRAIL
MARGAREE VALLEY AREA
A CANADIAN HERITAGE RIVER
SALMON MUSEUM & FISHING ▷
HISTORIC FISH HATCHERY ▷
CRAFT STUDIOS & GALLERIES ▷
GREAT FOOD & MUSIC ▷
ACCOMMODATION ▷

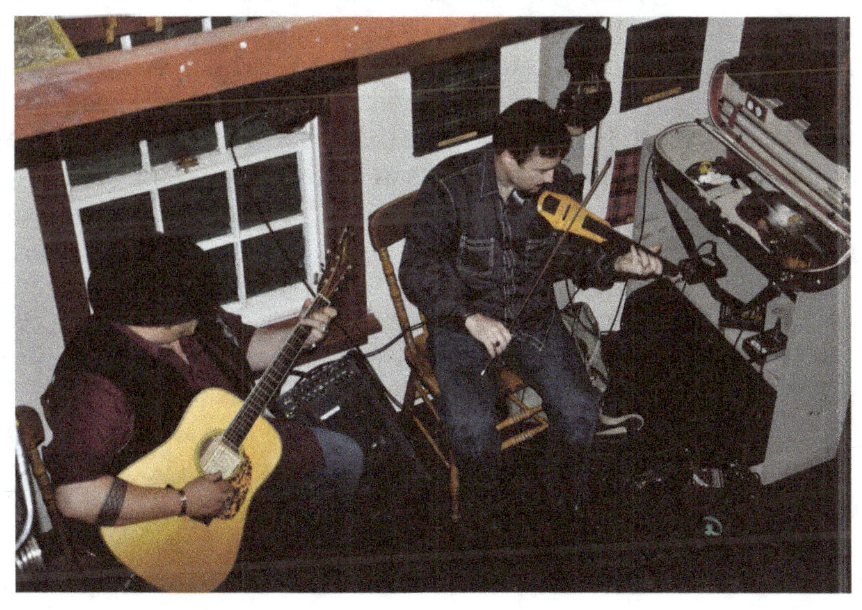

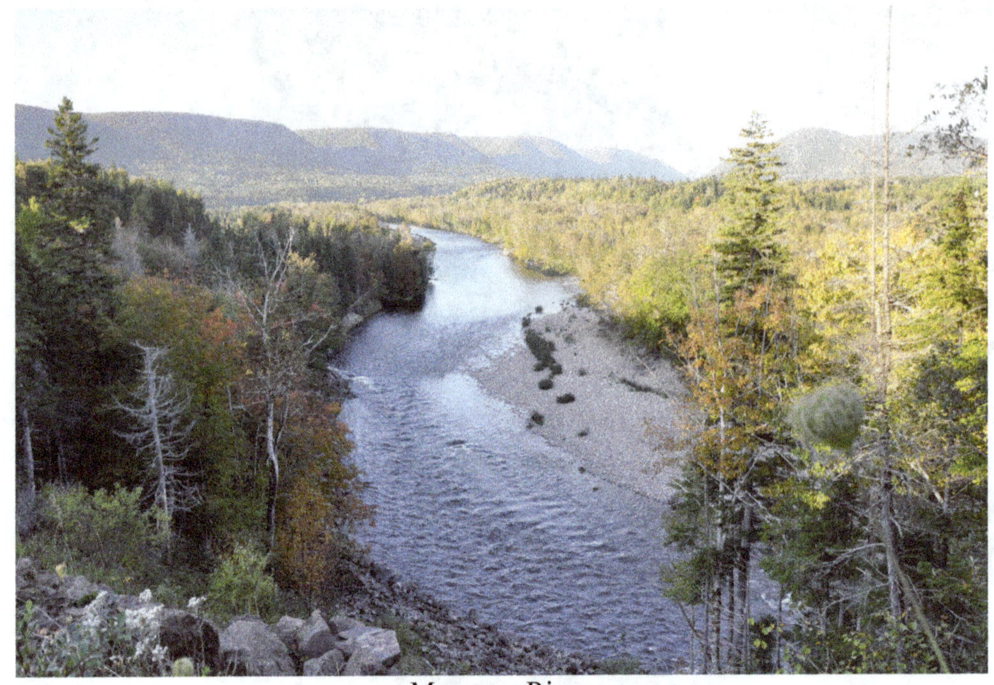

Margaree River

    As we approached Nova Scotia from New Brunswick, a nasty nor'easter began to
batter the northern coast with high winds and pelting rains. After the day's drive, we
slid into the historic Pictou Lodge which overlooks the northern sea to find respite
with their fine wine and food under the watchful eye of the lodge's huge fire-blazing
hearth. It was in this small village of Pictou that the mother ship Hector first landed
with Scottish settlers in 1773. The gusty winds and horizontal downpours pounded
the log-timbered building. It felt warm and safe to be snug and cozy in this
wonderful ambience and ruggedly tasteful setting. The next day we made our way
over the narrow Canso Causeway that separates Cape Breton from the main island.
The wind was still relentless, casting waves of ocean and mist over our vehicle
which made for a treacherous trek until we made it safely to solid ground. We sped
up Route 19 to visit the Celtic Music Interpretive Center in Judique, which proved to
be a splendid meeting place for learning about old and contemporary artists, getting a
bite to eat and taking in some live music. Further up the road we relished a late
lunch at The Red Shoe Pub in Mabou which is owned by the famous singing Rankin
family. It was the Rankin family songs that initiated us into the island's rural culture
on our first visit years ago, and we were disappointed to learn that they were not
performing on our trek through Cape Breton. So we slid in one of their CDs and
continued up the road harmonizing with them as best we could. By late afternoon we
drove into Margaree Valley and our lodging destination, the bucolic Normaway Inn.

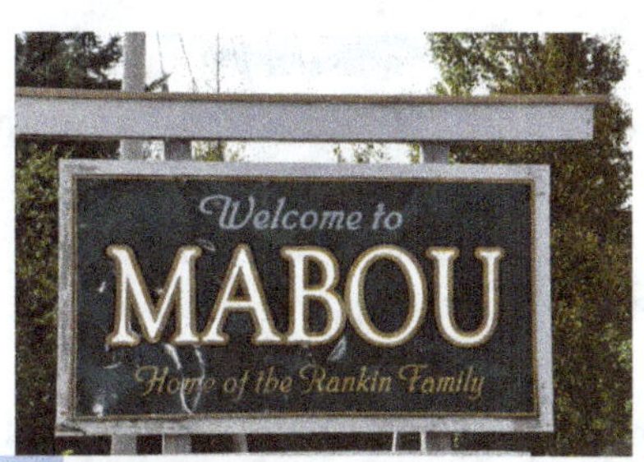

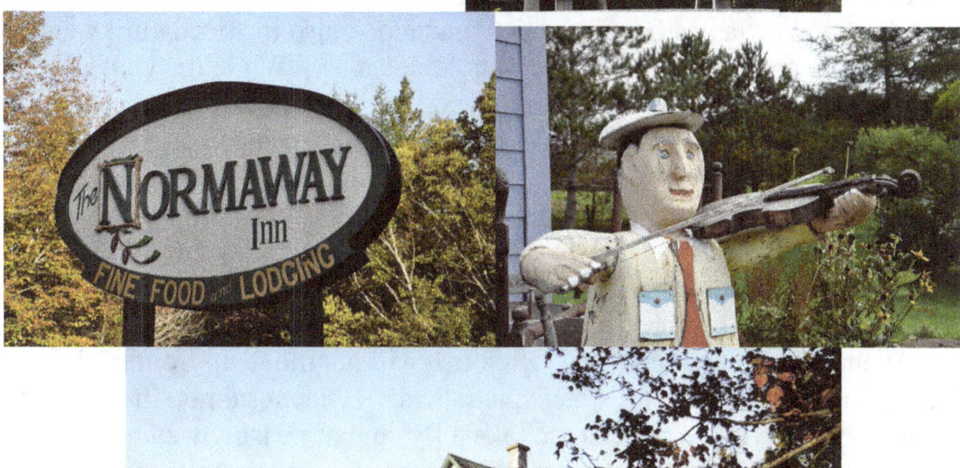

Innkeeper Dave MacDonald welcomed us in the reception room and gave us a rundown on the weather, musical-ceilidh concerts in 'The Barn' and the general fishing conditions. Dave is an affable, easygoing man with deep Scottish roots who loves Celtic music and does all he can to promote it. Most evenings he hosts musicians in the famous 'Barn' or in the inn's reading and correspondence room. One evening I hosted a conversation about fly fishing techniques and destinations with several of the guests, including some of the sports who were anxious to fish the Margaree River. Dave was kind to include my book *Life on the Fly* for sale in the inn's lobby. In the foyer we met fishing guide and president of the Margaree Salmon

Association, John Hart, and several fishermen that he was guiding. The weather was improving dramatically. Cool, crispy morning mists were swept away by late morning sun. The river conditions were suspect due to the heavy rains that had added inches to the river's flow. During the first couple days the water was indeed high and it was difficult to navigate many of the pools, but as the week went along, the river flow came down to fishable levels. We reviewed Mike Allen's 'New Handbook for Margaree' which proved helpful in locating and negotiating each pool. Mike's adaptation of James Grey's original handbook also included quirky anecdotes about the culture and personality of the Margaree Valley. While the valley had experienced heavy rains, the northern highlands were inundated with snow. As the snow melted, its waters came down into the valley and once again aided in raising the river's flow. Prior to the nor'easter storm, the fishing was good with several large salmon caught along the Margaree's 30 or more classic salmon pools. In fact 2011 proved to be the best salmon year in decades and this dramatic July influx of salmon was also experienced on the neighboring Cheticamp and Baddeck rivers. Praying for rain in late summer or fall is always a required tactic when planning a sea-run Atlantic salmon fishing trip. Often fish will not move up from the lower pools or ocean bay unless rising water spurs them. Resident salmon that have spent the summer in the river are reluctant to take a fly, and new rising waters often will get them to journey from their summer residences into new upper waters. In doing so they are more apt to take a fly when they are 'fresh' in a new pool or adjacent eddy. I surmise that the new surroundings ignites an internal desire to 'guard the territory' and that this instinct will often elicit a strike. It appeared that in our case, when all the prayers were tallied, too much rain prompted many salmon to tallyho to the far upper spawning pools that are off-limits to fishing. Pam and I were using floating lines with orange-colored shrimp patterns that may not have been getting deep enough to prompt a salmon up from the depths. Sinking lines, in hindsight, would have proved to be a better choice. Regardless, we saw a few fish, missed a number of close encounters and fished numerous pools over a course of 20 or so miles.

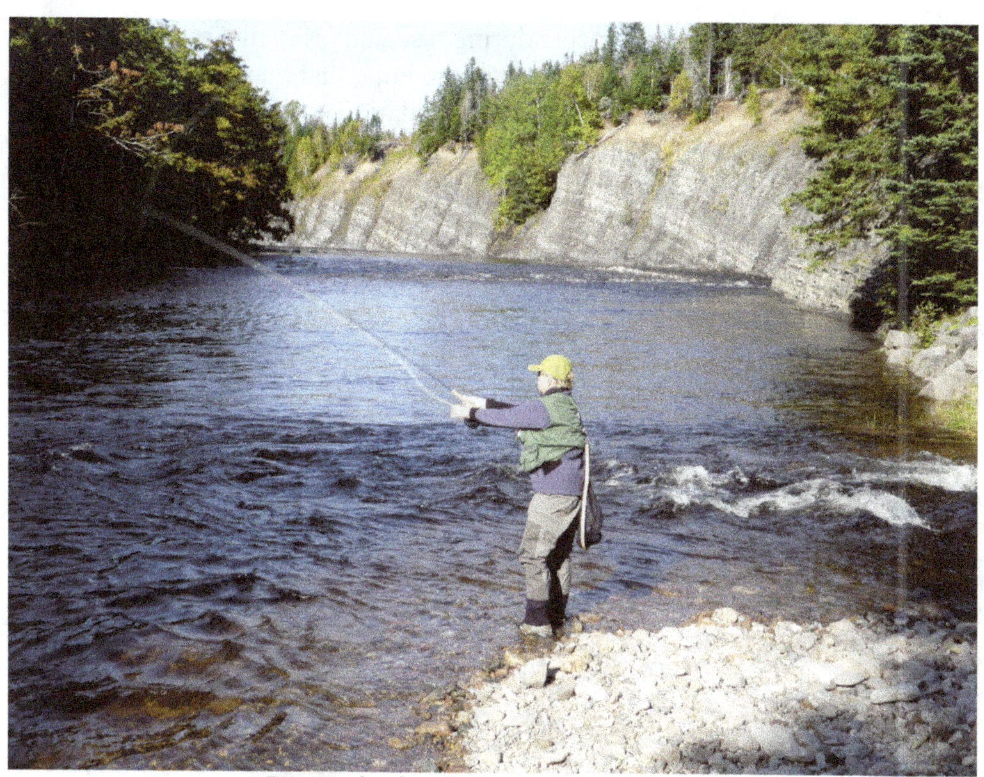
Pam casting into the majestic Hatchery pool

Hatchery & Museum

In between fishing excursions we made time to visit two favorite places — the Margaree Fish Hatchery and the Margaree Salmon Museum. The hatchery is Canada's second oldest, in operation since 1902. It has played a central role in maintaining the economic vitality and cultural heritage of fly fishing. Manager Sean Neary was very welcoming, giving a tour and explaining the manner in which the hatchery rears fingerlings (parr). Below the historic hatchery building is the hatchery pool where fall salmon brood-stock are collected in nets. An equal number of females and males are gathered — eggs are fertilized with the males milt in early November and incubated over the winter until they hatch in March. From this fertilization, Alevins are propagated and live on their yolk sacs for 4 to 6 weeks. Alevins transform into tiny salmon fry that are kept in outdoor ponds and raceways over the summer. During the fall, these more developed fingerlings (parr) are reared in long raceways and circular tanks until they reach 15 cm in length by October. Then finally they are released into the Margaree and other rivers, and typically make the rivers their home for one or two seasons growing in lengths to 25 cm. The fish that have transformed into smolts are ready to point their noses towards the ocean to

93

face uncertain and dangerous prospects during a sea odyssey that will take them off the Greenland coast. We cross our fingers in the hope that many will return to the river after a one to two year journey. Natural predation will take its toll on the salmon, but since great progress has been made to stop the commercial netting of these fish, many will survive to again swim the rivers of their birth and propagate their species.

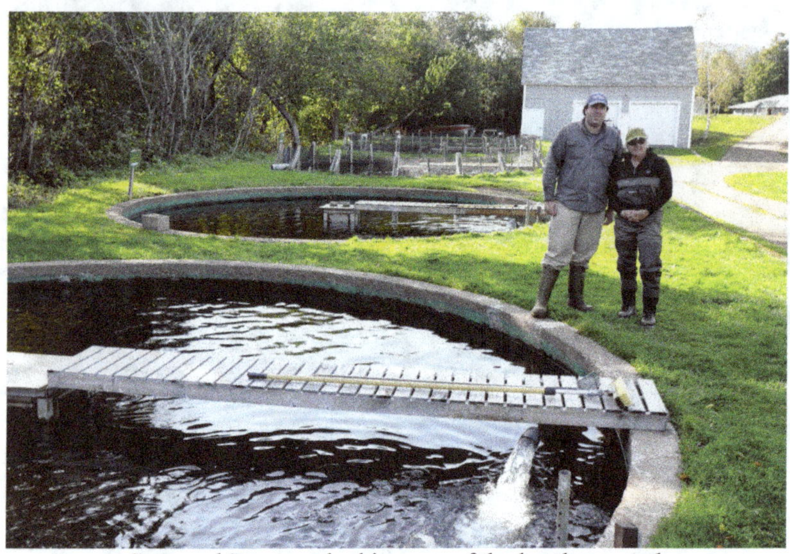
Sean and Pam overlooking one of the hatchery pools

Frances Hart has been the curator of the Salmon Museum for almost 40 years. She welcomed us in on our last morning in the valley after first placing the open sign in place on the doorway. Without doubt this is one of the finest and classiest museums dedicated to the display of historic fly fishing rods, reels, flies and related paraphernalia on planet earth. For the dedicated Atlantic salmon fisherman it is like a being a kid in a candy store. The presentation of art, fish mounts, books and personal notes left by famous anglers such as Lee Wulff, Ted Williams, James Grey and John Cosseboom are tastefully arranged for the fullest visual experience. One could spend days here investigating and delving into the great history of the Margaree River and learning about the men and women who have labored to preserve the river while eking out a living in such a remote setting. Frances was gracious in explaining various displays and pointing out newer donated acquisitions that she has mixed with artifacts that date back to the late 1800s. The museum has a number of books, pins, hats and art for purchase to help defray operating costs, and we obliged by acquiring some pins, a hat and a lithograph of a mighty salmo salar leaping up river by artist and museum benefactor Frank Burt Smoot (1906-2006). Frank was an avid fly fisher, writer, conservationist and humorist. He was a key figure in the annals of many Maryland conservationist initiatives. I'm a sucker for paintings of sport fish and anglers and being in this environment prompted me to once again acquire another hanging ornament to adorn our walls back home. "Tom, our walls are full. Where in the world are you going to hang it?" was Pam's comment as I stealthily convinced her about the importance of supporting the museum. As Pam nodded her head in with what I think was an okay jester, we bid farewell to Frances and the Margaree Valley.

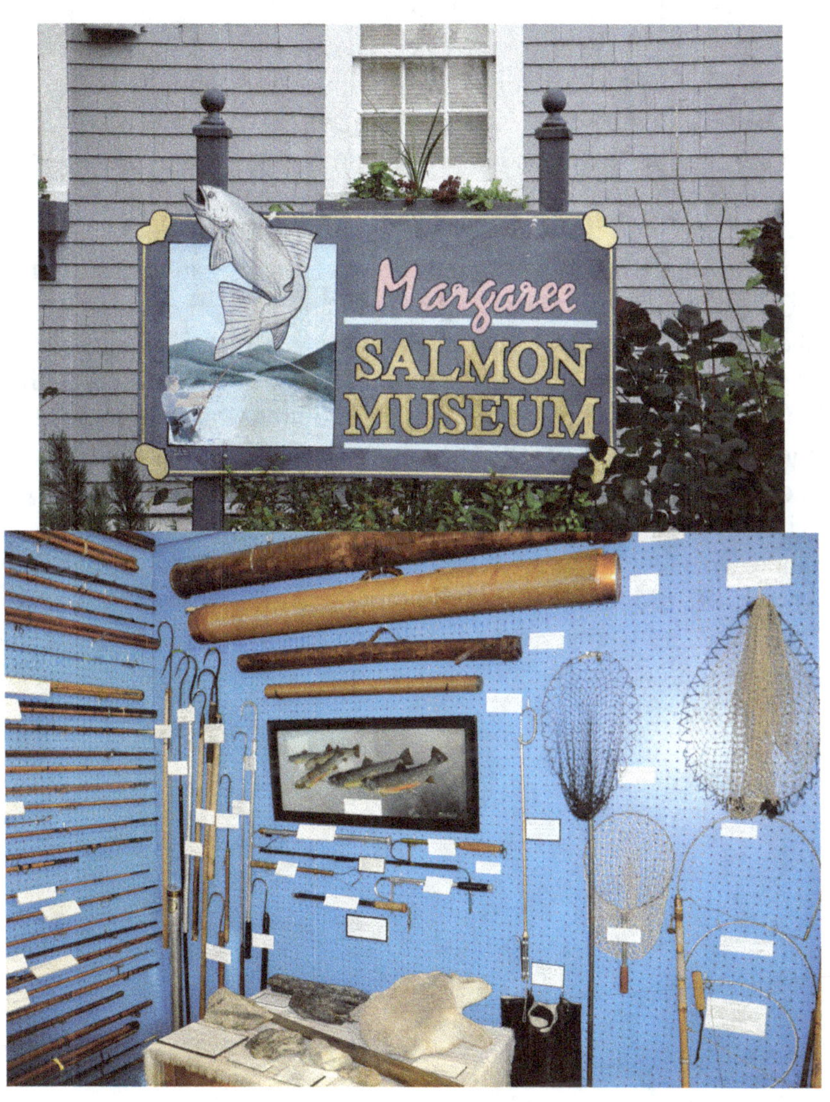

Margaree Salmon Association

John and Karen Hart have been the back bone and mainstay of the MSA for most of the last 25 years. John has reigned in the title of president while Karen steadfastly handles membership, correspondence and many behind-the-scene details and necessities in order to maintain the association's vitality and significance. Although I have been a life member of the association for a decade, I had not yet been able to attend the annual dinner and auction fundraiser at St. Patrick's Parish Hall in Northeast Margaree. This year was different. We were here finally to give support in person and to meet folks who journey far and near to lend a helping hand. After a fine dinner and desert, John Hart took to the podium and auctioned off rods, reels, lines, boots, flies, tying materials, clothes and hand-crafted objects for home and cabin adornment. A fine time was had by all and monies were raised to help with the Margaree River's ongoing conservation and preservation initiatives.

Before leaving Cape Breton we toured the sweeping ocean vistas of the Highland's Cabot Trail, hiked the Skyview Trail and learned more about the river's pools and their locations. One of these pools observed was called the Tingley Pool in the upper river sector. We first heard about this pool when talking with Merv Tingley who owns the popular Dancing Goat Restaurant that we frequented several mornings for great coffee, pastry and the best breakfast sandwiches we had ever sunk our teeth into. Merv and his family have deep roots on this land that borders the Margaree River and this inviting pool monogrammed in the family name. As is the case with land owners all along the river, Merv welcomed us to walk his land and try our luck fishing. We did so and even though we did not raise any salmon on that sun-filled afternoon, we learned to reach and cast into many of the upper pools. We put what we learned into our memory bank for use when we again return to seek the illusive silver swimmers.

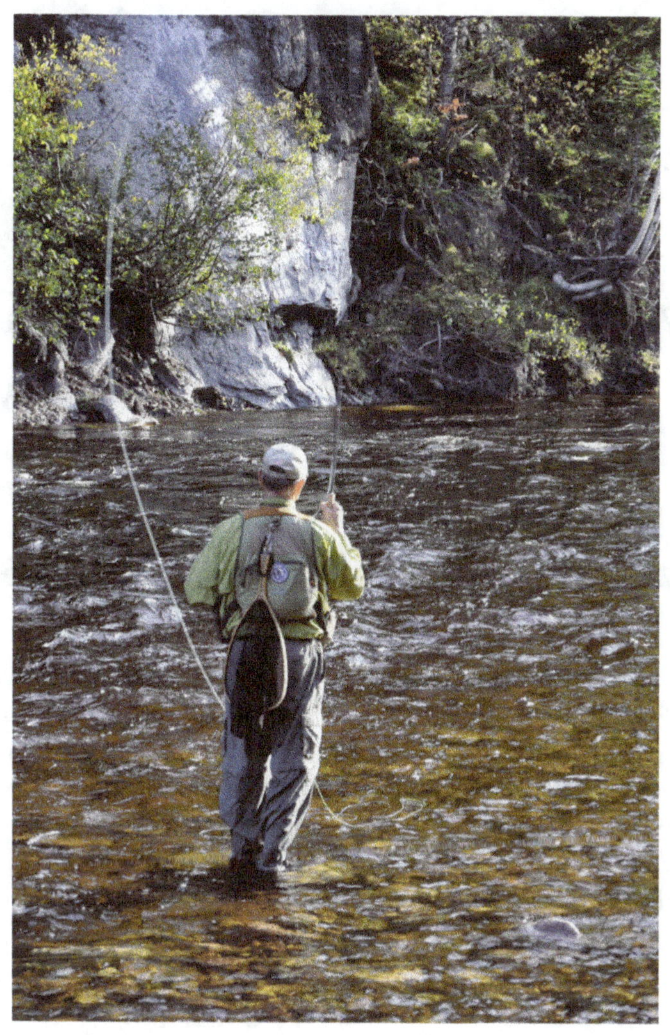

Driftless

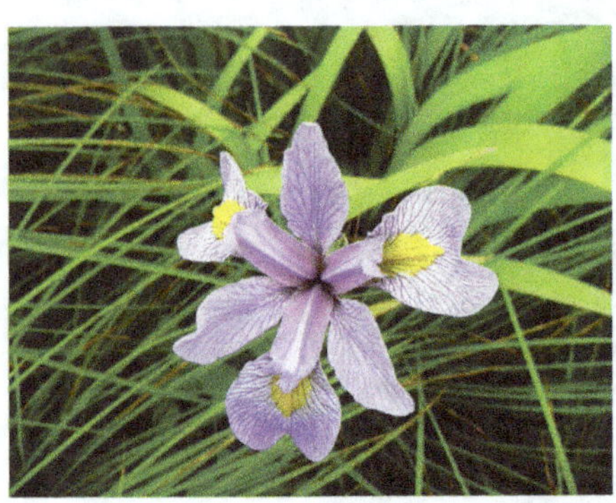

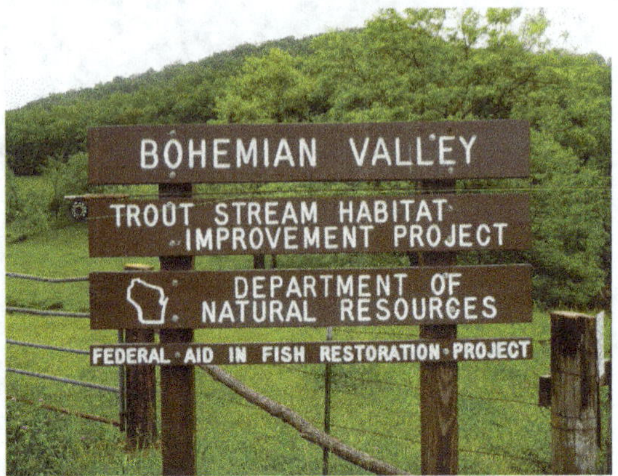

When I think about fly fishing I often focus and reflect upon the wonder of water and, more specifically, moving water. When I look upon the water I picture the fish finning in the currents waiting for their next meal and the other inhabitants that dwell behind and under the rocks and vegetation. Since ancient times the symbols of fish and water have been linked together to represent freedom, purity, mobility, determination, transformation, fulfillment and the flow of life. Truly all life is made from the magical mix of sun and rain, and I think it only natural that we are drawn to the realities and mysteries that await us in nature's wonderland. As fly fisherman, we seek to hook up with what this moving water is holding for us. Is there a hatch going on? What fly from the countless thousands of insects flying or nymphs emerging from the river bottoms will work in the next hour as we ponder what to tie on to the end of our leader? Our eyes are affixed upon the water, its flow, the insect activity and observing those slots where wild fish are likely to hide and ingest easy meals flowing by. Our minds and bodies are transfixed and drawn to these ancient elements that have and will continue to sustain life.

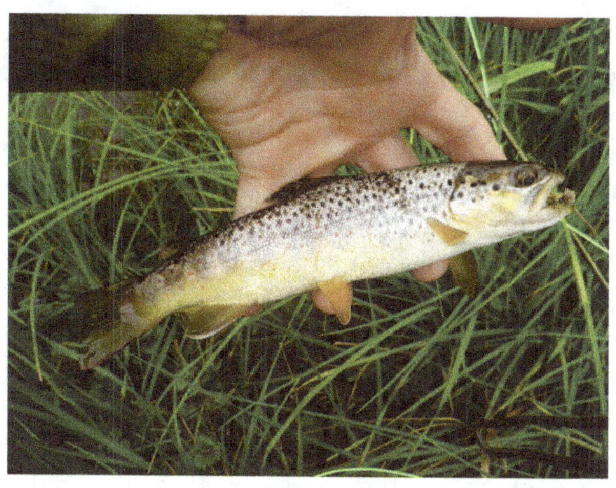

In May, 2012 my wife Pam and I were transported to the "driftless" corner of S.W. Wisconsin on the invite of our friends Ned and Elizabeth Bacon and Ned's parents John and Liz Bacon. Living in the Midwest for over 40 years, John and Liz have fished this Kickapoo area for many years and wanted to give us a potpourri experience covering eight rivers in four days. John and Liz picked us up at the Chicago Airport. John drove the nostalgic hippy-like 1990 Westfalia van with Ned and I in tow, while Liz, Pam and Elizabeth sped off in Liz's sedan. The weather was warm and the days were sunny except for a few intermittent afternoon and evening thunderstorms that raced quickly through these lush farming valleys. The Bacons arranged convenient country lodging in a 100-year-old German farmhouse a few miles from the town of Viroqua. John and Liz gave us an overview of the area and its many spring creeks holding healthy numbers of wild brown trout.

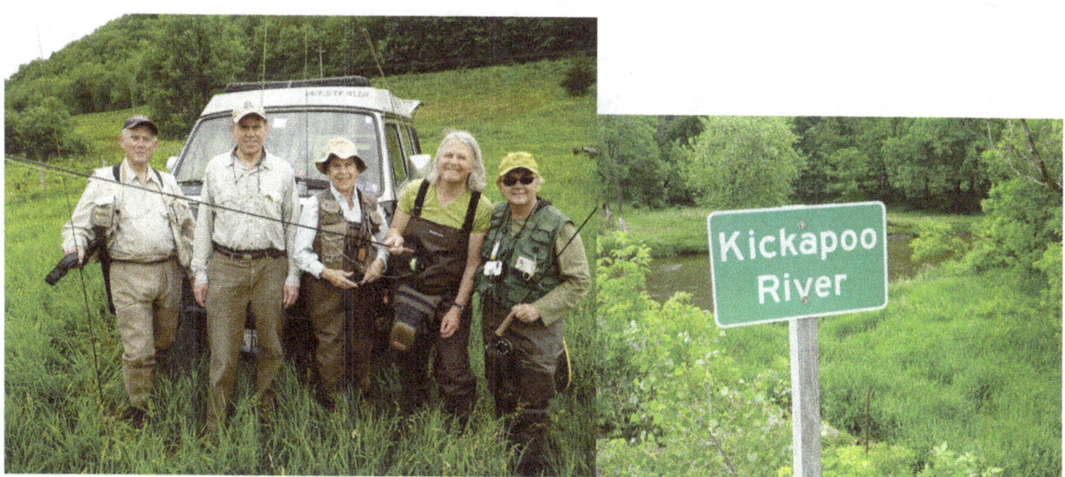

John, Ned, Liz, Elizabeth, Pam

In four days we managed to fish the following creeks: Elk, Reeds, Bohemian, Bishops Branch, South Fork Bad Axe, Hornby, Tainter and Big Green. That was a lot of fishing to bite off and often there were rivers that were hot with action that we didn't want to leave, but leave we did to experience other nearby streams. These limestone creeks are generally not wide, but many have deep pools and hidden passages where wary trout take up residence. Over the course of the past 30 years, several Trout Unlimited chapters have merged their talents to restore and create trout havens on these primitive waters. On many of the river bends 'lunker structures' were engineered into the banks to allow fish to seek shade and safety. The streams are full of trout of all sizes with Bad Axe holding some of the largest due to its wider girth and deeper pools. Casting a fly on most of these creeks is relatively easy as these waters weave and curl their way through pastures dotted with Holstein, Angus and Hereford cows that eat most of the vegetation along the banks. Pam and I had luck tying on a variety of flies to lure hungry trout. Sulfurs, Drakes, Blue-Winged Olives, Tan and Cream Caddis Dries and wets in sizes 16 to 22 did the trick. We used a combination of 7 to 9 foot tapered and straight 3 to 5 lb leaders affixed to floating lines. Our arsenal of rod sizes ranged from 3 to 5 weights.

After enjoying a morning plodding the waters of the Bad Axe, I got the hand wave that it was time to venture over to Hornby Creek. I never like to be pried off a river that was producing so well with much more water to cover, but another creek was calling to us. After a quick, windy drive, we quickly split up along the Hornby to try our luck. All of these streams are cold and crystal clear, and the trout were easily spooked as we attempted to gain some higher ground to peer into the pools. I was creeping up the river bank trying to keep a low profile when I noticed many trout risings below a riffle emptying into a pool that was not more than four feet across. My second cast got caught up in a fence post just below the main activity. I cursed at the wind as I slowly worked my way over to uncurl the leader at the back of the pool. My hope was that I wouldn't totally screw up the feeding frenzy. As it turned out, luck was with me as the trout kept up their feverish quest of ingesting tiny caddis flies. With virtually every short cast, a wild trout would smash my imitation. In the next 35 minutes I hooked and released not less than 10 handsome trout. Every day, every cast, and every challenge proved to be a special treat, and I was amazed at the large numbers of fish that live in over 200 miles of these pristine spring-fed trout waters. The Bacons were most gracious with their hospitality and educating us to the wonders of the many trout filled creeks of America's Driftless territory.

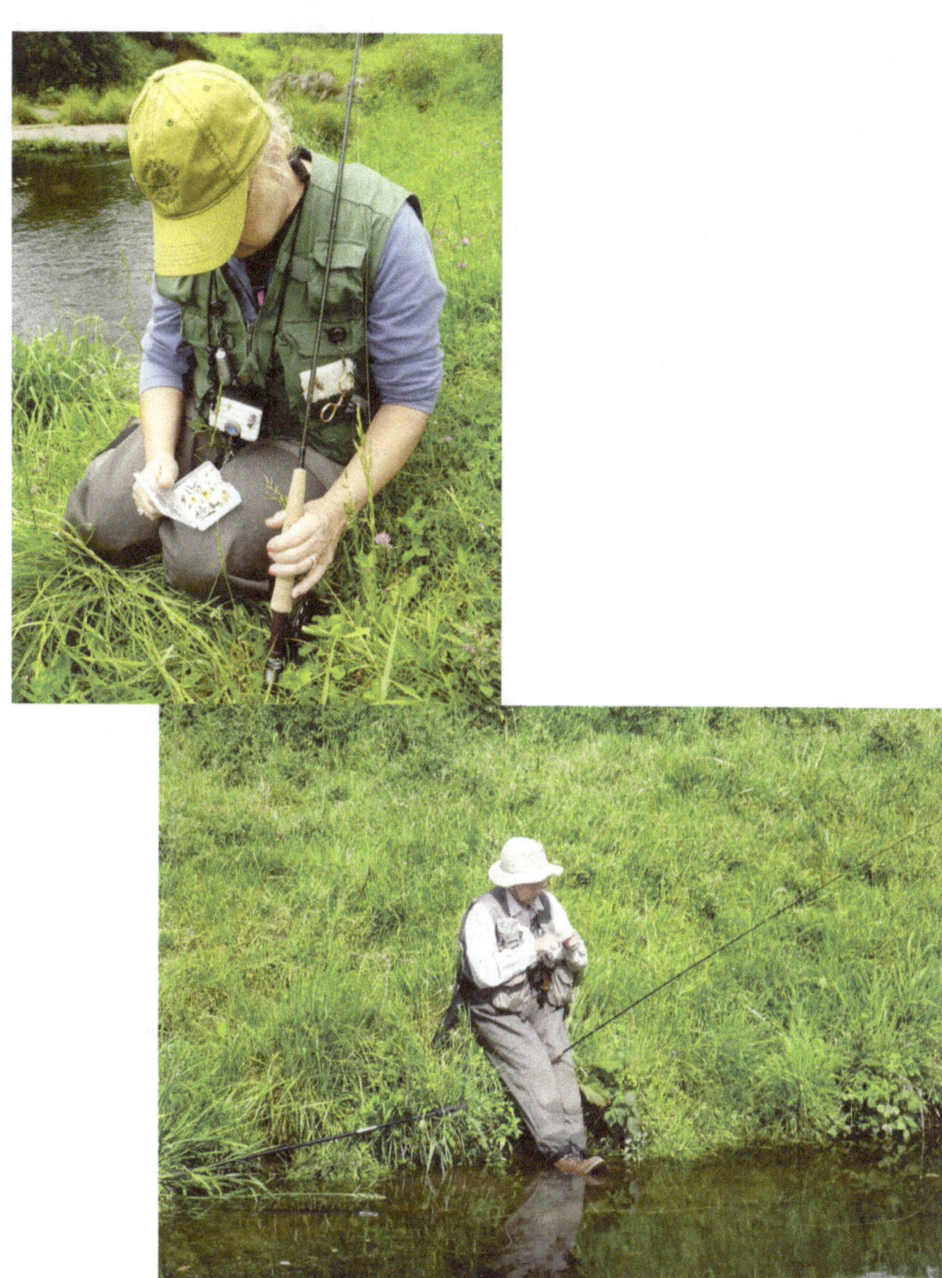

Pam and Liz finding the right fly

101

The Quest

By a stream never faltering on
    its chosen path,
        chiseled through ages long gone by,
        at home within a world of wild
    natural sights, is where I choose
to make my promised land.

There, in oaken smells of spring
      with green-forested hills
      diligently embracing
    that chosen stream,
is where I set my mind to dream.

The rippling raging river
      holds beneath its silver-clad waves
      the sole sincere desire of my quest,
    the most worthy of them all:
the cagey trout.

Stealthily,
    I approach the riverbank,
      cast my line into a likely pool
      and let the fly meander where it will,
    in hopes of luring a native brookie
from his bed.

Chickadees arrive
    to inspect the scene,
      distant owls cry out their mating hoots,
      the sun drops slowly to the hills,
    breezes do their rustling
in the trees.

A sly doe
    sneaks out from the bush
      and feeds on clover in a nearby field.
      Her spotted fawn
      soon joins her by her side
    and frolics in the grass
when all seems safe.

I soon forget
    the object of my quest
      as nature does her thing to all I see.
      This peaceful setting puts the mind to rest
    and gives the soul
a reason just to be.

Suddenly,
    my rod feels a jolt,
      line unwinds briskly from the reel.
      Instinctively, my focus reappears
    as the brookie and I are joined
to one another.

The rod tip bends to meet his every thrust
    as he boldly tries to break
      our ephemeral bond.
      Soon my net enshrines
      this speckled being;
    he sparkles as I lay him softly
in the grass.

Quickly,
    I release the hook from his lip,
      hold him with two hands and feel his life,
      then gently place him back
      into the stream—
    the place of his beginning
and that of mine.

Sometimes when I am lying in my bed,
    thinking of my quest so pensively,
      I wonder if I really hooked that trout
    or
      if that trout had put his hook
in me.

Jerry Johnson
Author of
Up the Creek Without a Saddle and ***Noah's Song***
www.VTPOET.com

Mass Wanderings

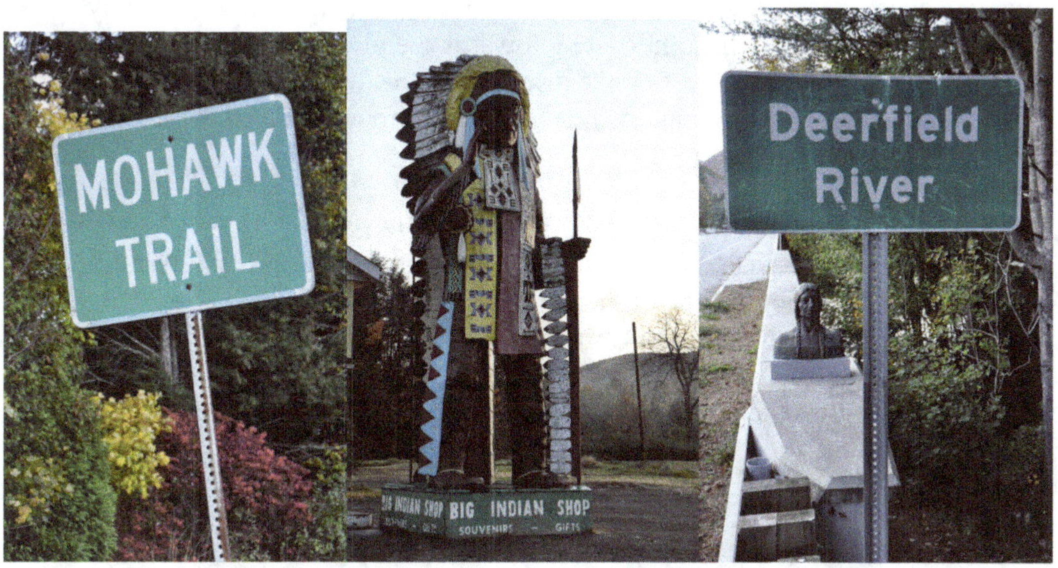

As a life-long resident of Massachusetts, I have often set my sights on day journeys to many of our trout and salmon waters. I am particularly enamored with the rivers and streams of the pastoral and forested western part of the state. One would be wise to acquire *An Angler's Guide To Trout Fishing In Massachusetts* published by the Mass – Rhode Island Council of Trout Unlimited. Contact the Central Mass Trout Unlimited Chapter #148 for a copy. One of my favorites for consistent catches in ice-cold, clear water is the Swift River. The river can be accessed from many locations. Its flow begins at the 'Y Pool' just below the Windsor Dam outlet of the Quabbin Reservoir. This is a very popular catch and release destination pool by many anglers, since many large trout take up residence just below the dam. From here and continuing downstream for many miles anglers can sight-fish for brown, brook and especially rainbow trout. Sometimes Salmon will oblige with a smash of the fly and lively tail-escalating leaps. Most of the river banks are high, so it is easy to view feeding trout maneuvering their way towards their next meal. Insect hatches are plentiful, so it is always prudent to study the insect activity before proceeding to cast a fly with the hope of matching what the trout are feeding on. Since the water is translucent-clear and because the fish see many offerings, thin 6X or 7X leaders are most often recommended. Since there are many stocked and holdover fish, each section of the river holds numerous trout.

Hence, when starting to fish an area where fish have been sighted, it is best to have patience and try several fly patterns before moving up or down the river. The fish are very active in this river and they dart up and down, over and across in their quest to ingest the next best meal. Persistence in one location usually rewards the angler. On numerous occasions I have netted many fish from one pool location before moving to another section of the river. Other pools and riffles can be found by following River Road south from Route 9 towards the town of Bondsville. Heading south further on Route 181 takes one to a section of the Ware River—another excellent trout river that flows many miles, and is composed of east, west and main branches.

Other trout waters of note include the Westfield, Housatonic, Deerfield, Green, and Millers Rivers. Of these, the east, middle and west branches of the Westfield River and several sections of the Deerfield River are two of my favorites. On a number of occasions my daughter Karin and I have float-tripped the Deerfield River with Tom and Dan Harrison of Harrison Anglers. Floating with Tom or Dan is an excellent way to learn the rivers and enhance the fly fishing experience.

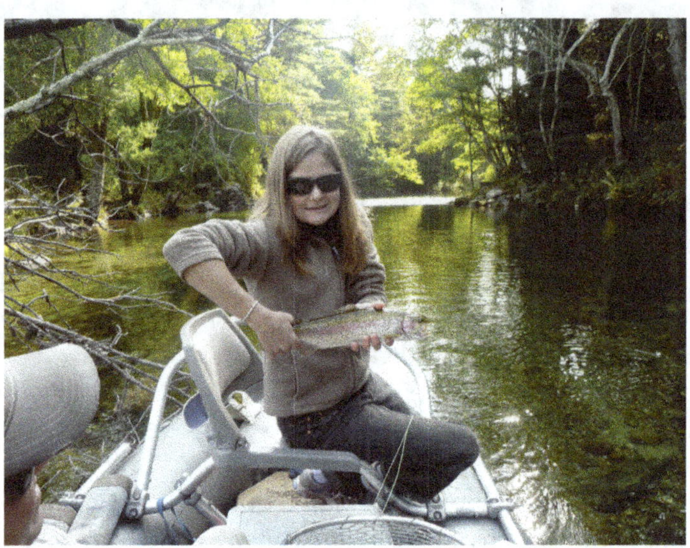

On the Deerfield many fly patterns work well including nymphing with a pink San Juan worm attached to a lower caddis fly in a variety of colors. Dry fly sizes vary between size 16 to tiny 24s. Some of the best fly fishing exists on rivers with man-made dams. The waters released from the Swift and Deerfield River dams provide clean and cold flows all summer long. This consistency in water quality provides ideal habitat for abundant insect activity and subsequent healthy fish. The dam release flows on the Swift are consistently the same, whereas the cubic feet per second (CFSs) on the larger Deerfield can change at a moments notice. Usually the

Deerfield flows are lower in the morning until about 10 am, and then pick up from there-sometimes significantly. Before venturing out to wade the river, it is always wise to check the scheduled water flows since high water can sometimes make it difficult to maneuver safely. High water flows usually do not negatively affect boat floating.

Before venturing forth view the Waterline webpage www.h2online.com.

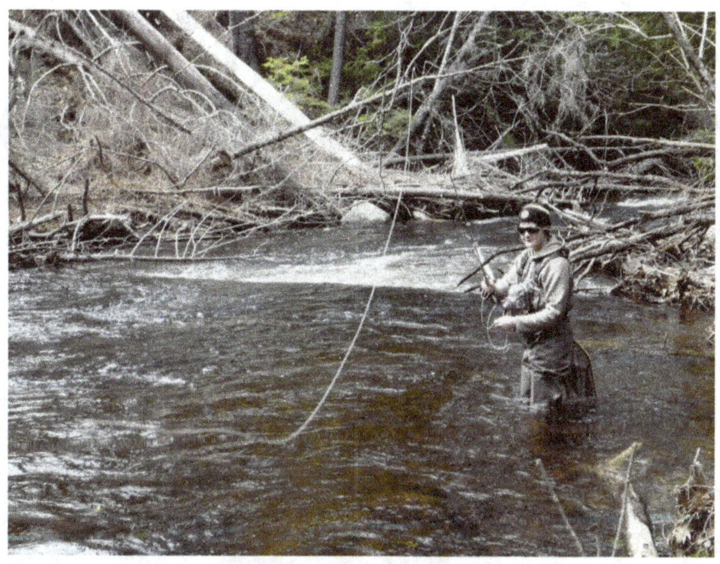

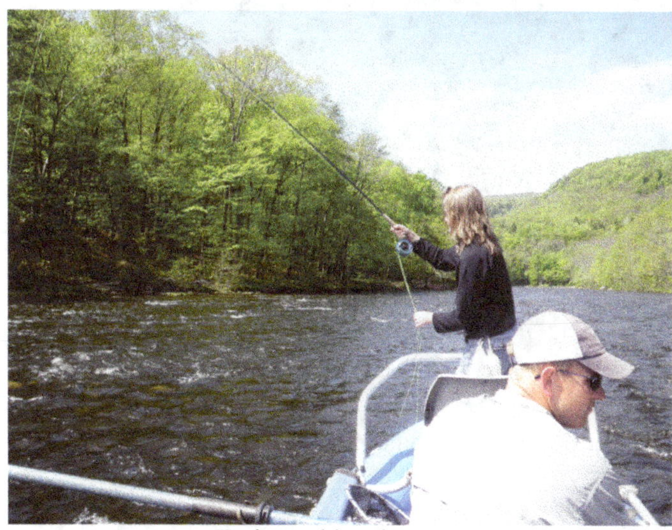

Karin working the water

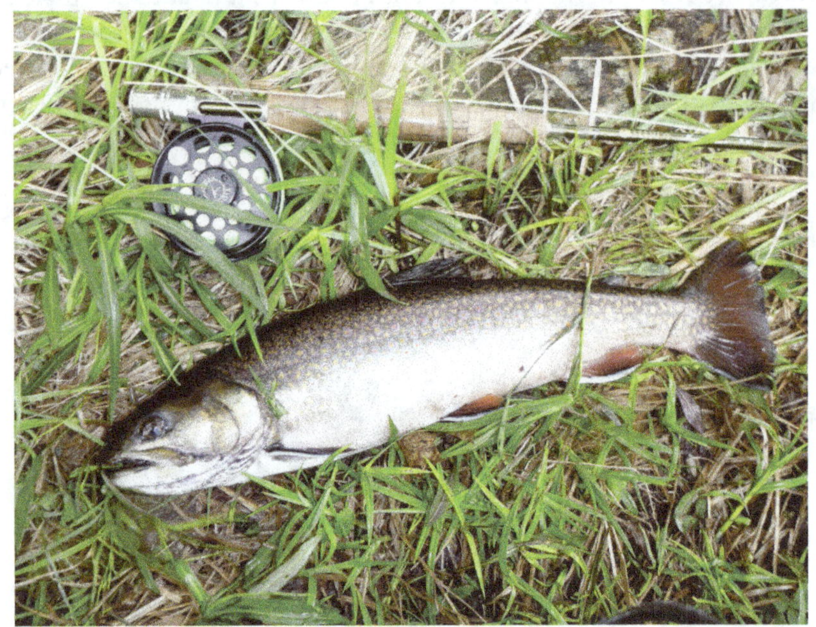

Nice Brookie Result

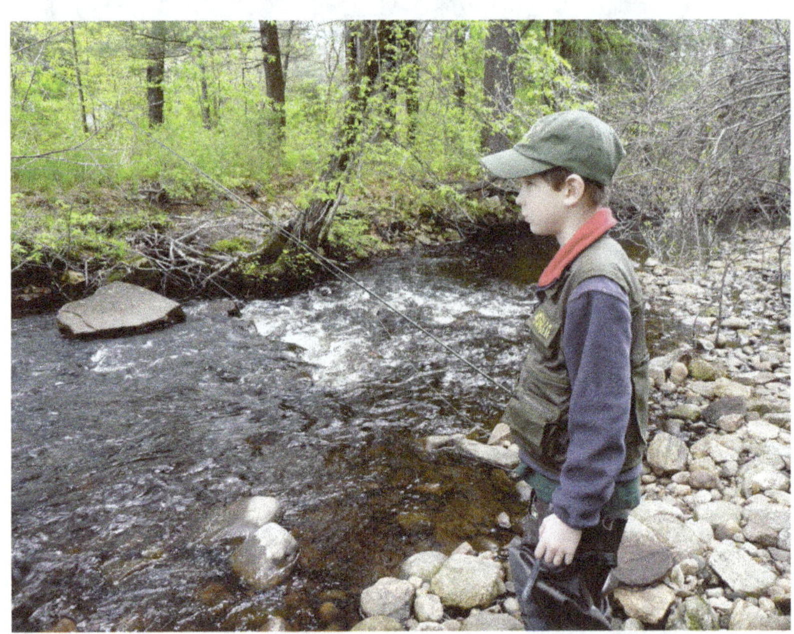

Grandson Gabriel looking for brookies on small central Mass creek

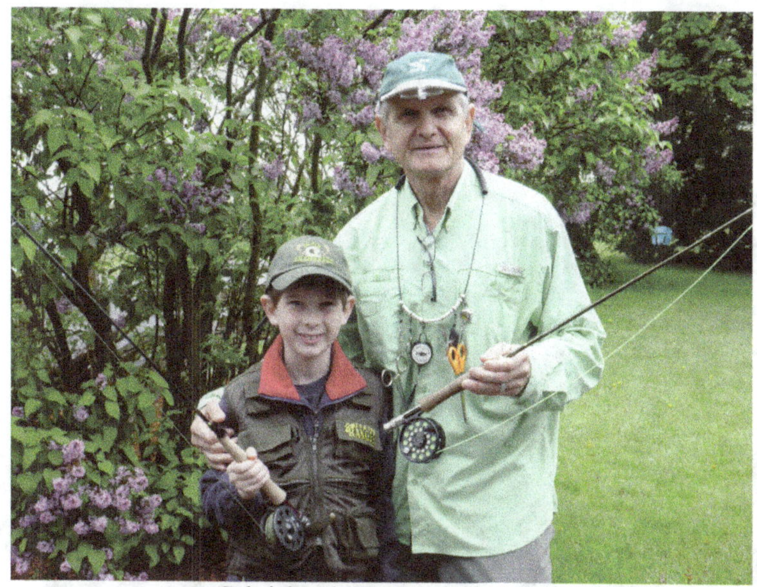

Gabriel and Grampa ready to go

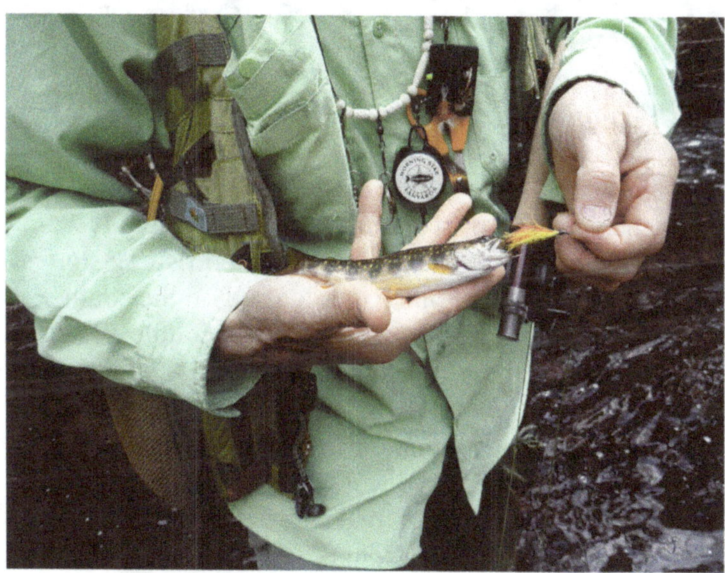

Gabe's brookie hit a Mickey Finn

Chapter 15

Newfoundland Journey

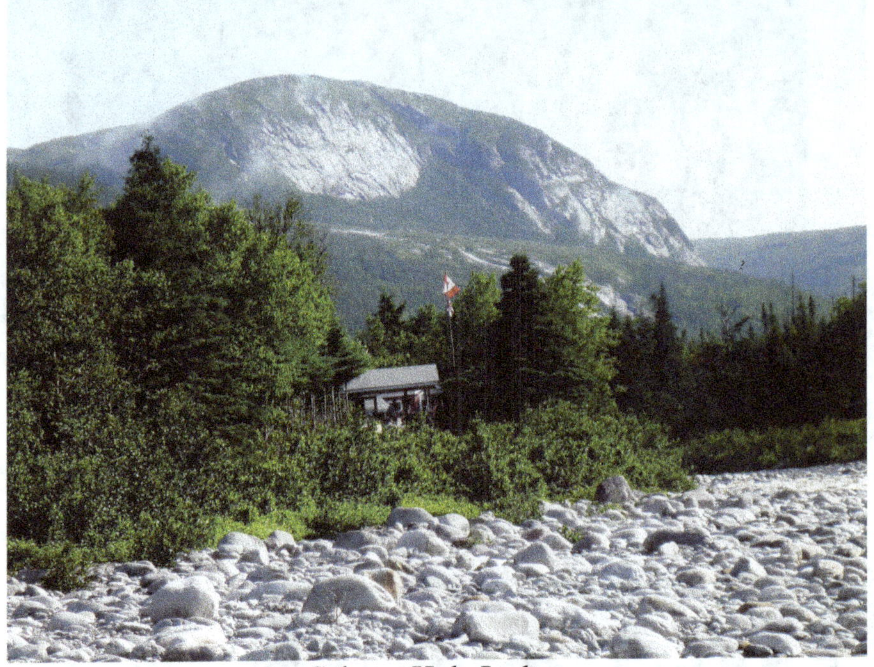

Salmon Hole Lodge

Every March several of our family members venture to the New England Atlantic Salmon Federation (ASF) dinner and fund raiser in Freeport, Maine. Several years ago at the event we met brothers Jim and Russ Staples. As we shared fishing stories they told us about their exploits at the distant La Poile River located on the southern coast of Newfoundland. It wasn't long before they invited me and a couple friends to join them with their friend Doug Garcia, and so we did. In mid July, 2014 an old college buddy Dan Stark and friend Terry McGovern joined me at Jim's cabin in northern Maine for wine, dinner and making last minute preparations for our trip the following day. I had no idea how much work Jim and Russ did to prepare for this trek further north. I soon learned why this pilgrimage they made every year was something that was rooted in their DNA, in their hearts, in their very souls.

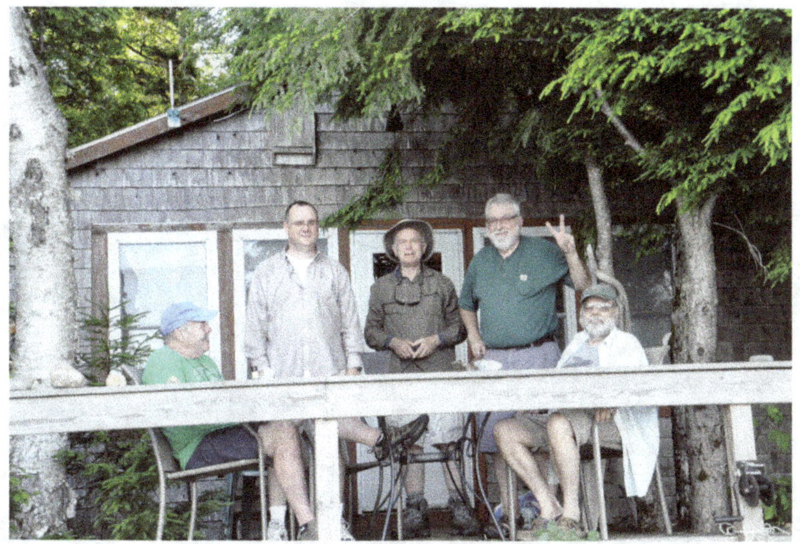

Terry, Doug, Dan, Jim, Russ at Maine camp

The Staple brothers have been fishing the La Poile River for over 30 years, having been introduced to the Salmon Hole Lodge there by their dad Walter. Walter wet his first fly line there thanks to the invites by Duncan Smith in 1980 and later by Duncan's son Scott. In 1998 Walter wrote *The North Bay Narrative* which details the history of this area, its peoples and their work over the course of 150 years. It's an account of a small band of families lead by the Farrell and Strickland clans eking out a living in the remoteness of this often hostile environment. They were a ruggedly independent people who toiled long hours each day with their hands and keen minds to support themselves.

They built a village, a school, and sawmill to facilitate their craft in building skiffs and schooners for the local fishing fleets. There was an abundant amount of spruce, fir and yellow birch trees that were cut up and down along the river's edge. The felled trees were driven up by ox or slid down to the sawmill using the energy provided by the rivers flow. They would get by with a few cows, sheep, a small garden, hunting for moose, caribou and fishing for trout, salmon and cod. This life in North Bay Village slowly faded away in the 1960s as families moved away to find more opportunities and easier lives. Most of those who remained in the area relocated to the village of La Poile where they fished the ocean for cod and found employment as fishing and hunting guides for sportsman who were discovering this territory full of game and fish.

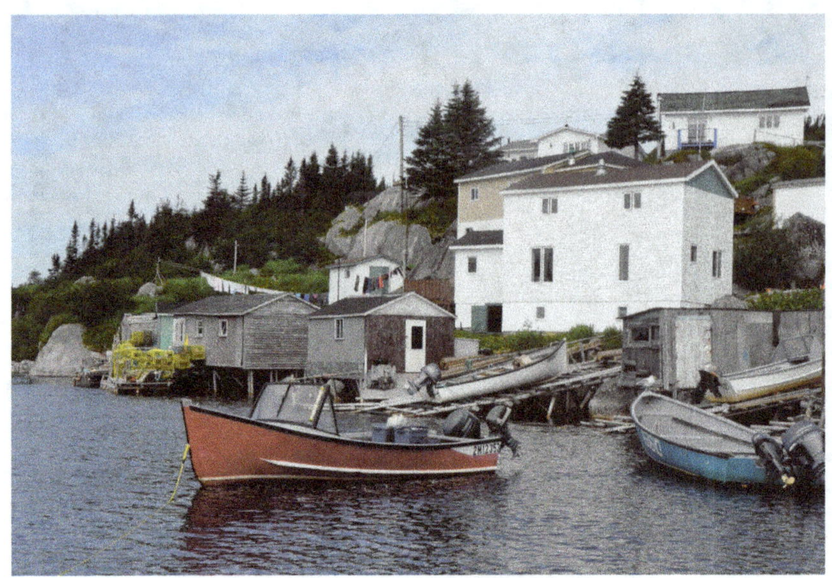

La Poile village with Alex's smaller boat

Since there are no stores for 60 miles, each fishing group must bring in their own food and drink for a week's stay, including fare for the guides. Months in advance Jim tabulates what the menu will be for each day's breakfast, lunch and dinner. Over the course of several weeks he purchases all needy goods and loads them into Russ's pickup truck. After we arrive at Jim's camp we load more provisions into the truck and our fishing gear into the Staples SUV. We leave early the next morning so that we can make the evening 100 mile ocean ship journey from North Sydney, Nova Scotia to Port aux Basques, Newfoundland. After driving 500 miles we are tuckered out and ready to hit the sack. We park the vehicles on the ship, and find sleeping quarters in the small upper cabins. With little elbow room, but no complaints, our eyes quickly closed on our pillows. Arriving in the morning on the big island, we wheel off the vessel and head east along the southern shore for about 30 miles, at which time we come to the roads end at the coastal village of Rose Blanche. Here we are greeted by a 40 ft. diesel powered fishing boat. We unloaded the gear, transported it into the cargo section of the vessel, and parked the vehicles. Once aboard we continued east along the coast for another 25 miles, arriving in the fishing village of La Poile. We were greeted here by head fishing guide Alex Chant, his wife Eileen, and guide Sidney Chant in their smaller wooden craft. Again we re-loaded our stuff on to their boat as it eased alongside. Alex and Sidney have been guiding here for over 40 years. Heading out of the La Poile harbor we took some photos and motored around the rocky high contour of the headwaters towards La Poile River valley—9 miles north.

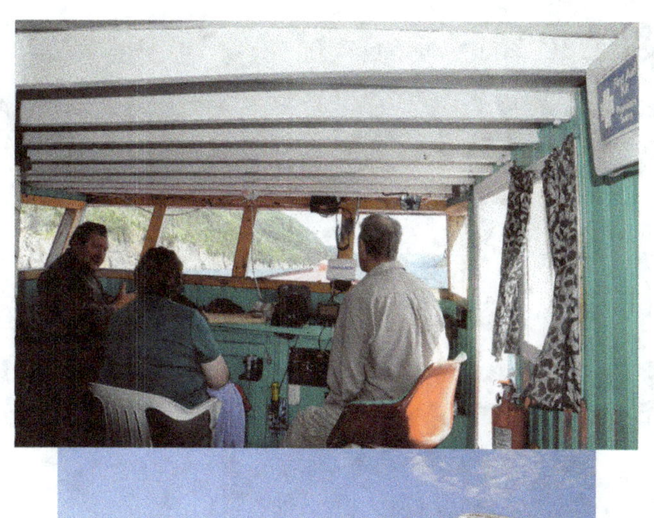

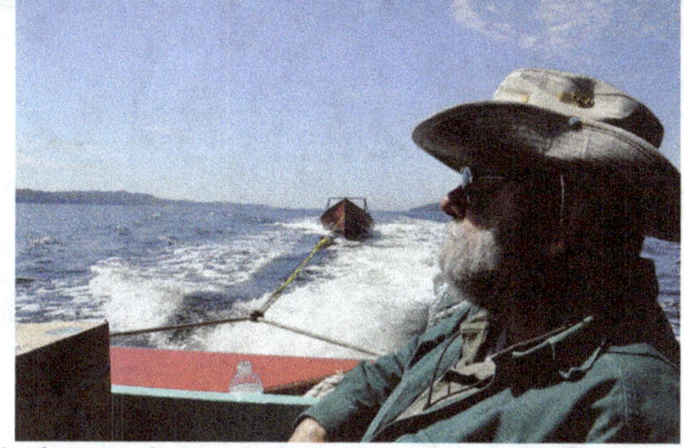

Sidney, Eileen and Alex steering towards La Poile River while Russ takes in the views and sun

   As the valley narrowed we finally made it to North Bay harbor, where we again one final time transferred our gear, which was becoming heavier by the moment, into yet another smaller skiff a short distance from shore. Once finally ashore we were greeted by a few of the natives who only summer here now. The provisions were loaded into two old wooden carts that were in due time motored up river to Salmon Hole Lodge by two equally worthy antique tractors. Jim and Eileen road buck side on one of the tractor seats while the rest of us slipped on our back packs and began the 3 mile hike up to camp. As it turned out, it was no easy walk in the park. Several times we needed to wade across the swift currents of the river and attempt to follow a rocky path hardly worn down by tractors that have wheeled this way for many decades. Black flies would play havoc with our necks if the wind inside the river's islands died down, but once again back in or along the river, the steady winds kept those nasty critters at bay. Finally we limped into camp, shed our sweaty clothes, showered down and prepared our gear for the afternoon's fishing. In short order the tractors loaded with the rest of our provisions and food arrived. An ample and hearty lunch was soon prepared by the able hands of Alex and Eileen.

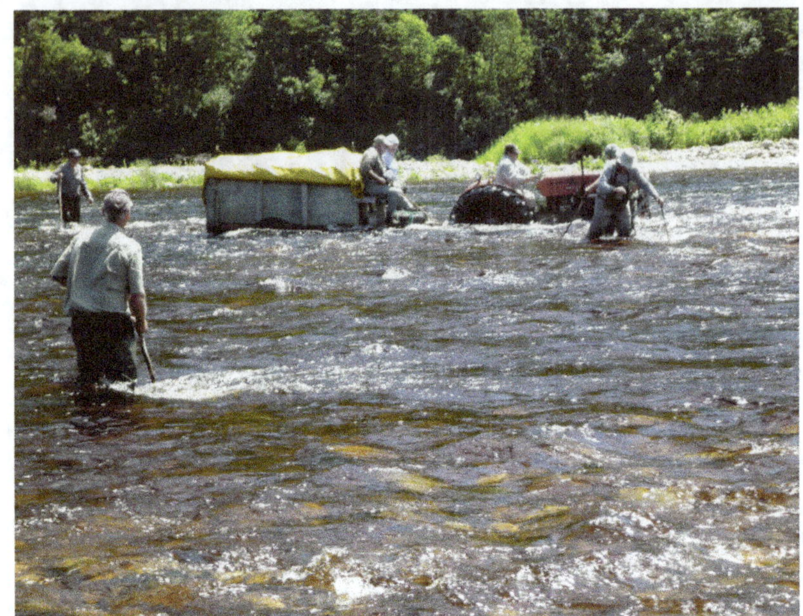

Treacherous river crossings were the order of the day. Hold on!

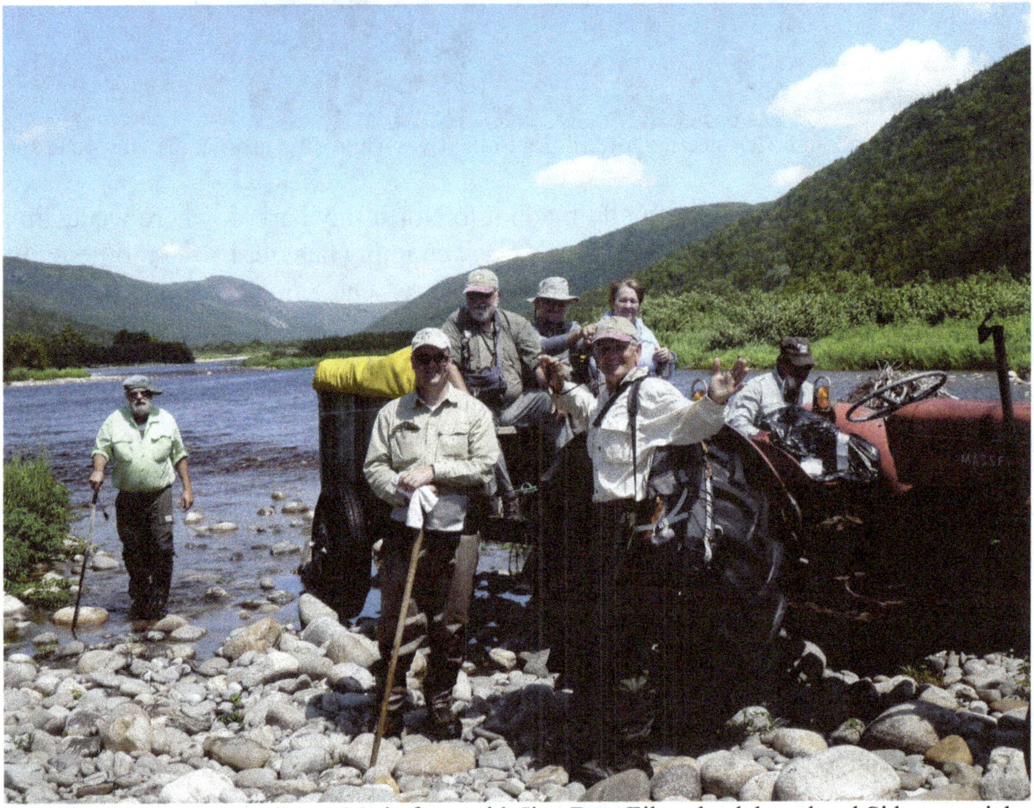

Trekking to camp - Russ, Doug, Me in front with Jim, Dan, Eileen buck board and Sidney on right

With renewed energy we were off to explore the salmon pools up river. The
weather forecast was promising with clear skies, cool nights and comfortable
temperatures during the fly casting days. The river conditions were not the best with
relatively low water flow, which does not prove beneficial for prompting salmon in
the bay to nose their way up river to the pools. But, with 32 pools to choose from,
we all had ample opportunity to explore and fine tune our fly lines to well defined
salmon holding lies. We all had come with a liberal supply of flies. These included
wets like Green Machines, Blue Charms, Rusty Rats, Buck Bugs and Ally's
Shrimps. Top water dry fly favorites chosen were Bombers in various color patterns,
Wulffs and Butt Bugs. However, as it often proves with many fishing adventures,
the local guides often have their own fly concoctions that work better. Certainly this
was the case at Salmon Hole Lodge. Sidney and Alex Chant had a large selection of
what they referred to as the go-to-fly simply named the Green-Brown Bomber in
rather small 16-18 sizes. It has a deer haired green front, brown back with a white,
fuzzy tail. It is spun all around from front to back with a brown wing feather. It
became my go-to-fly for the week. The long and deep Bathtub pool just up river
from camp proved to have the best salmon holding and taking spot that we could find
during this low water week. In the evening Sidney positioned me on the river bank
above a large, submerged boulder where several silver swimmers were positioned
one behind the other on the far side of the rock. After several casts with the
diminutive bomber dimpling over the fish, a white flash rose against the side of the
fly. This was certainly an interested salmon, but there was no strike. So I rested the
pool for a few minutes to make certain that the fish would settle back into its lie. I
then proceeded to drop the next presentation just a few yards in front of the fish, and
allow the fly to skim over the fishes view. Bang, "Fish on!" I yelled. My fly line
screamed off the reel as the energized swimmer made several long runs and leaps
into the air. It's always a balancing act of how much pressure one should exert on
the fish in a pool filled with sharp-edged rocks and fast currents—enough force is
necessary to hopefully control the fish while also allowing a loosening line when the
fighter takes off like lightning and goes airborne. The salmon often wins by
throwing the fly or breaking the leader off in the rocks. This time, however, I was
lucky and brought the salmon into Sidney's awaiting net. All the guys had luck in
this pool during the course of the week. Alex and Sidney had us tromping miles up
and down the river, working us over and around boulders, and peat bogs that were
located inland just over the rivers crest. Let me tell you, each day brought with it
one good workout that burned all the calories we could muster. Eileen's great
cooking with ample helpings kept us going and renewed us for the next day's hiking
adventure. At camp when our eyes would rest from the river and look around at the
beauty of the valley and its mountains, we were greeted by a cow moose visit one
day and sightings of a herd of caribou on a treeless ridge several miles away. Doug
cited the tradition of climbing the mountain across from the camp and erecting a

white flag at the top. So one afternoon he took on this obligation and after several hours we could see the flag flying in the wind. Great job, Doug!

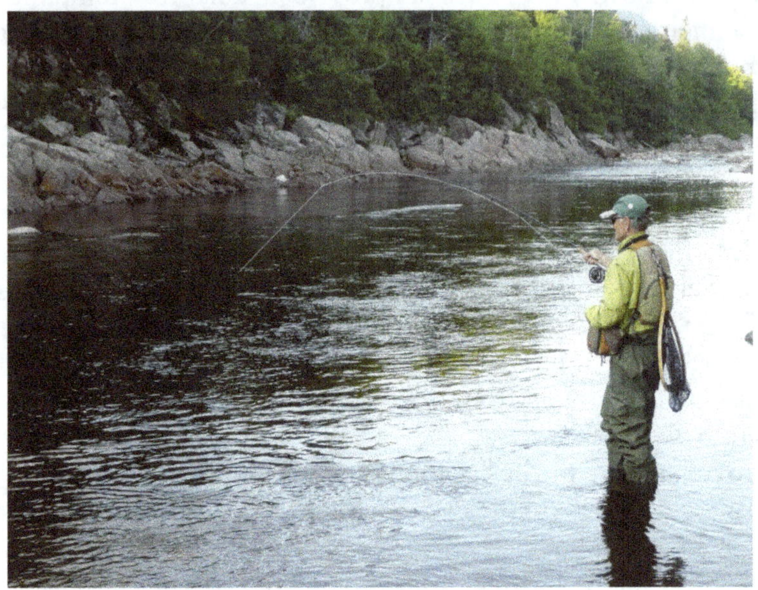
My first fish on at Bathtub Pool

Towards the end of the week I was working the lower end of the Camp pool. At the back end of the pool just before the water thinned out there were several large rocks adjacent to a couple of deep water pockets. With the tried and true small green and brown bomber I began to fly cast diagonally across and over this water. This episode turned out to be one of my most interesting and satisfying salmon experiences. After several casts a salmon rose and put his nose on the fly and disappeared. I rested the pool. Again on the next cast the salmon came up and basically just played with the fly with his nose bumping it several times as it danced across the back of the pool. My anticipation and attentiveness were on high alert as this visual encounter heightened with each succeeding cast. Finally after about a half hour of this nip and tuck game, I rested the pool and my nerves for several long minutes. I had all but conceded that this salmon was never going to take my fly, and that it just wanted to have fun playing with me and my elevated anxiety. Ok, just one more try I mused. For whatever reason the salmon finally latched on to the bomber, swam up the pool like a torpedo and leaped 6 feet into the air. I should not have been taken by surprise, but I was. That's always the case with salmon fishing—just when you let your armor down they surprise you with a bang, splash, and leaps, as line screams off your reel. You can never figure them out and I guess that's one of the reasons salmon fishers like me pursue salmon—for that unexpected encounter at that singular, spontaneous, surprising moment in time. These are what good memories are made of. I recollect those special outdoor experiences that linger in my mind—the ones that stay secured within, so I can reminisce and share them. By week's end we head down to North Bay to stay one afternoon and night in the Chant's summer place before departing for home. The sun was blazing against a bright blue sky as the gentle, cooling winds of the ocean curled up through the valley and beyond. For us it was a time for needed relaxation and to feel the distant pulse of this once thriving fishing and ship building village. Most houses sat empty, echoes of the past as grass and long-ago planted flowers mixed with the wild ones firmly held their ground.

As we depart we read what Pearl Farrell penned in the late 1940s:

"Now it's a lonely, lovely place where wildlife runs riot and a few houses, one being our original home and another our grandfather's home, still stand, looking lost and lonely among the trees and flowers that are run wild."

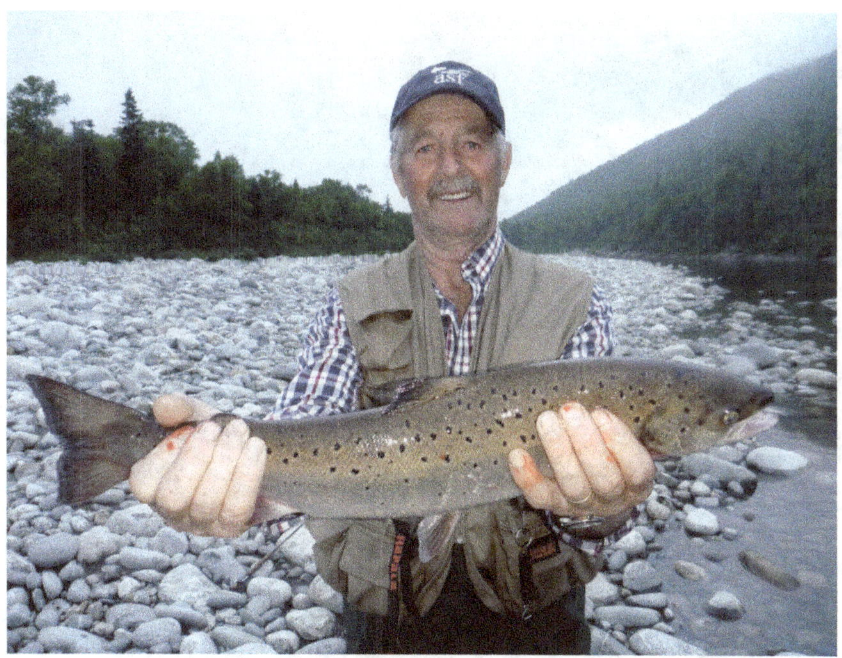

Alex with my fish at Lower Camp Pool

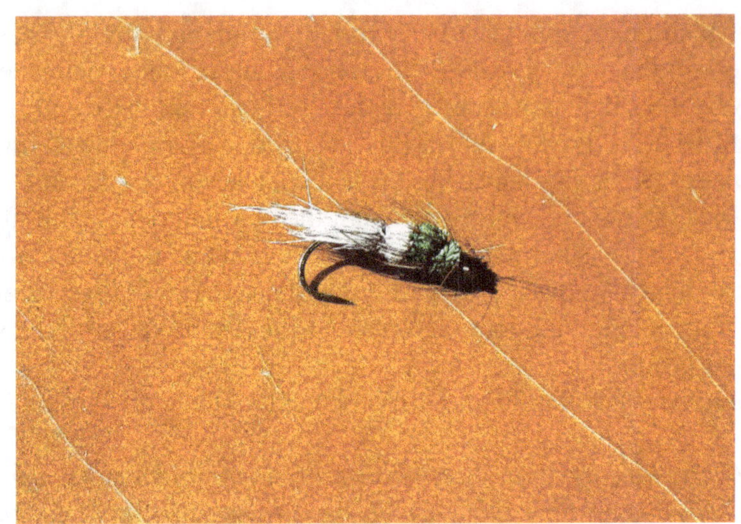

The Bomber that did the trick

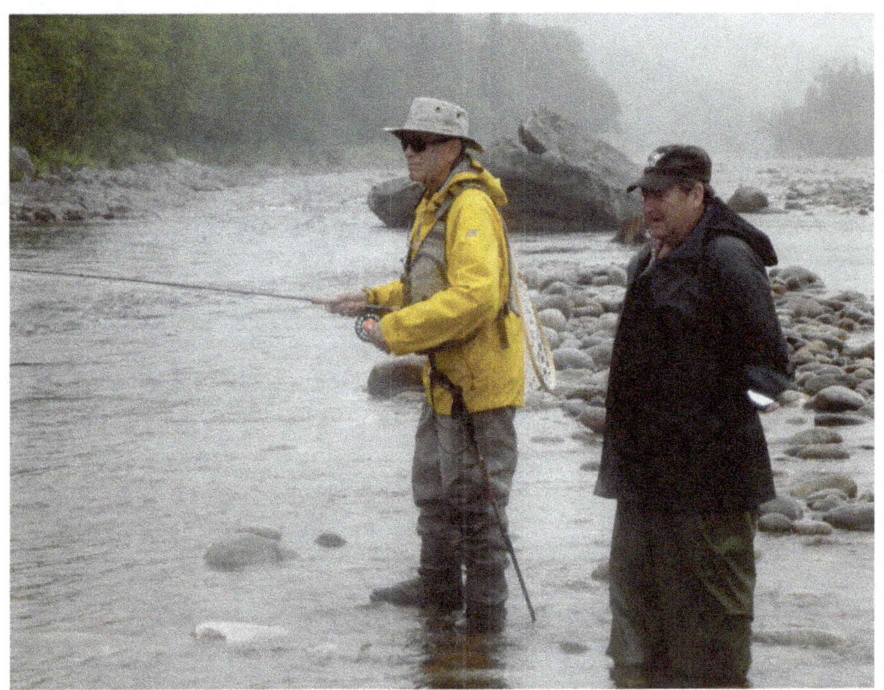

Dan at Split Rock Pool with Sidney

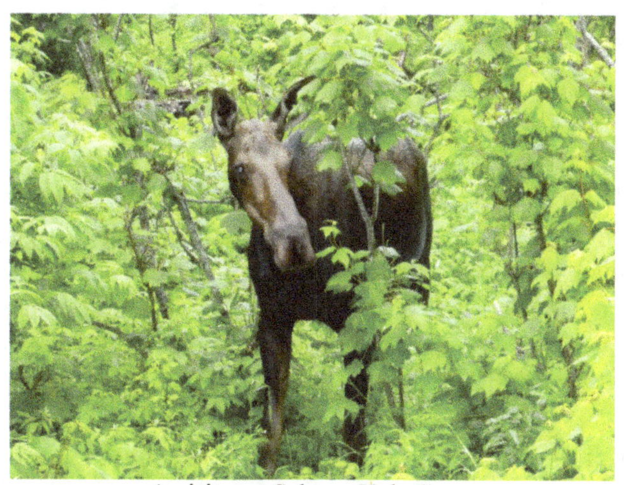

A visitor at Salmon Hole Camp

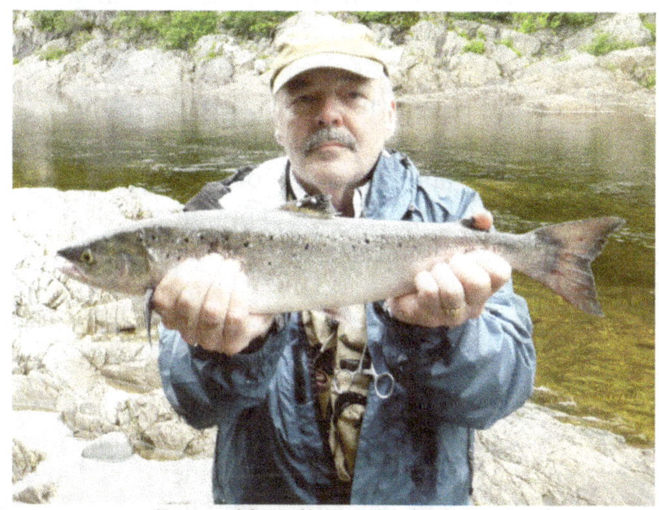

Terry with 'grilse' at Bathtub Pool

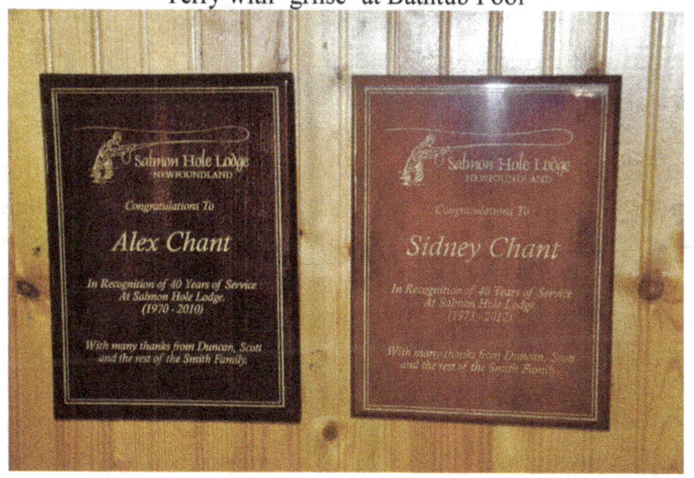

Chapter 16

Downeast Maine Renewal

The upper northeast quadrant of Maine has a number of rivers that once held good populations of Atlantic salmon. These include the Narraguagus, Pleasant, Machias, East Machias and Denny's rivers. At a St. George River Chapter Trout Unlimited meeting in Camden, Maine, I was in the company of Jacob van de Sande. He is the hatchery manager at the Downeast Salmon Federation's East Machias Aquatic Research Center, Columbia Falls, Maine. Jacob, DSF executive director Dwayne Shaw and many volunteers are revolutionizing propagating methods that will hopefully lead to salmon recoveries in these rivers. As the evening's speaker Jacob outlined the most recent progress at the hatchery, combined with other conservation initiatives needed to restore salmon runs in these rivers. Salmon hatch as young alevins that evolve into fry, then parr, then smolt. As smolt they leave the rivers of their birth, head northeast off the coast of Greenland for one to two years and then return as grilse (young salmon) to spawn. On average only 1 to 2% of each year's river population return to the rivers of their birth due to the hazards met along the way including predation, disease and high-seas commercial netting. Unlike their Pacific salmon cousins, most Atlantic salmon do not die after spawning, but have the innate capacity to reproduce and go to sea and return a multiple number of times as larger specimens.

For many years salmon rivers have been stocked primarily with salmon fry. The results have been discouraging with less than 1% of salmon returns on most rivers. With the combined efforts of the North Atlantic Salmon Fund (NASF), Atlantic Salmon Federation (ASF) and other conservation partners, the Downeast Salmon Federation (DSF) has transformed its hatchery techniques to mirror those that have been used successfully at the river Tyne's Kielder Salmon Hatchery in England. That hatchery's manager Peter Gray is mainly responsible for the recovery of the Tyne river salmon runs, using techniques that in his words produce "salmon that are little athletes. They must have the size, muscle texture and survival-of-the-fittest instincts that will enable them to swim to Greenland and Iceland and then come back to reproduce in your rivers." So instead of stocking baby fry, his success has been to stock larger, stronger parr in the fall that have a greater ability to eat natural food and avoid predators. Under Peter Gray's guidance at the East Machias hatchery in 2012 and 2013, the hatchery was re-tooled with proven incubator boxes that better mimicked real salmon redds (gravel beds where salmon lay their eggs) and holding tanks where the baby fry are fed and grow stronger with varying degrees of water flow rates. In 2013 102,000 eggs were received at the hatchery with the number expected to increase to about 400,000 eggs over the next two years. These applied techniques appear to be the last best hope for salmon recoveries for Maine rivers.

Habitat restoration in these watersheds is also of vital importance for salmon survival. The East Machias river system is still relatively pristine and is characterized by deep forests, swamps, ponds, lakes and tributary streams. However, 200 years of logging has impaired the landscape with logging road culverts, remains of log drive dams and outlet dams on several lakes. Many culverts do not allow the free passage of fish to move up and down rivers. Logging dams impound water that can create heating zones which salmon need to avoid. Outlet dams on lakes also impair fish passage. Project SHARE has invested over $300,000 in the East Machias watershed to rectify these problems. Other supporters include the Maine Forest Service and the Maine Department of Marine Resources. Their restoration efforts include the positioning of large wood in tributaries that have lost their natural cover, and replacing road culverts with waste block bridges. ASF and DSF have also built a new $100,000 Denil Fishway below the Crawford and Pocomoonshine Lake. This passage will allow the free upstream migration of anadromous salmon, river herring and eels. A recovering ecology factors in the historical relationships between salmon and other aquatic species. Salmon restoration must include multispecies management to be successful. Water PH levels are also of utmost importance to mitigate. PH levels below 5.6 are detrimental to the fish's gills functioning. To increase the PH to 6 or better, clam shells are being placed upstream, and the results have been encouraging. Maine is fortunate to have an abundant amount of discarded shells and therefore it is economically feasible to implement their life sustaining lime to offset the effects of acid soils and acidic rains.

www.mainesalmonrivers.org

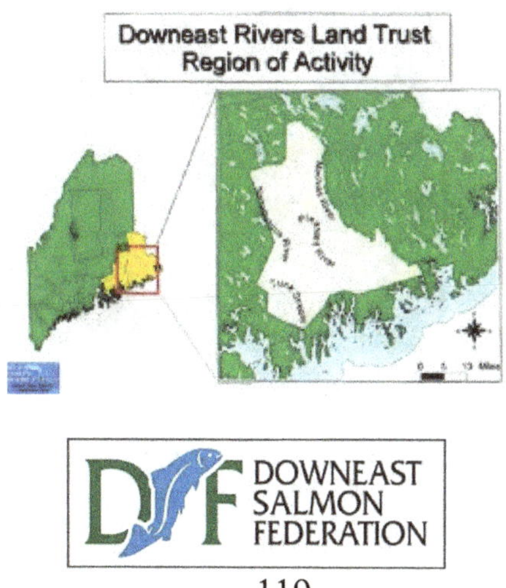

Chapter 17

Difference Makers

I have been fortunate to meet people who have made a positive difference in this world. There are thousands of notable people that have done great and remarkable things, and who have made this world a better place to live in for others. Sometimes a few of these individuals are recognized on the national and international level. More often than not they are missed in the flux of a media chasing the melodrama of the day, or the often boring hyperboles of the week. When we think of legends we are often drawn to people who have done great humanitarian deeds, those who have been accomplished in the arts, sports, and individuals whose heroic and adventurous lives leave us spellbound. Some are household names. However, most often they live unceremoniously and humbly in the background. The difference makers I speak of are those folks whose actions and thoughts have impacted the lives of so many in a positive way through preservation efforts, education and sports, and using their talents to make this world a cleaner and safer place for its inhabitants. We all have our heroes—the grade school teacher who turned us on to reading, the father or uncle who introduced us to fly fishing, the grandmother, who taught us how to keep our heritage alive by teaching us how to bake Swedish coffee bread – the mother who took us under her wing — that particular person whose life of giving has inspired us to the degree that moves us to emulate them. In the course of growing up we all need positive role models to help us make better choices as we enter adulthood and beyond. Here are some of my heroes.

Orri Vigfusson

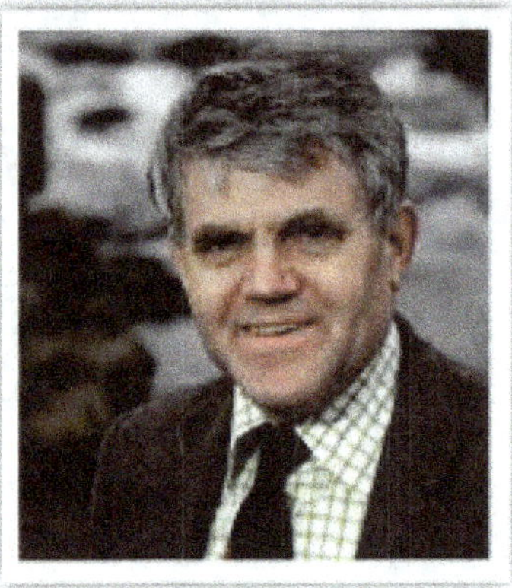

In a previous publication I wrote about Orri Vigfusson of Iceland who fathered The North Atlantic Salmon Fund (NASF), and who won the coveted *Goldman Environmental Prize* in 2007. His quest and success in saving the North Atlantic salmon from extinction is unparallel. He has orchestrated multimillion dollar buyouts, moratorium agreements with commercial fisherman, and fleets who were extracting over 600,000 tons of Atlantic salmon off the shores of Greenland and other ocean sanctuaries. Buying these netting rights allow these fish to propagate and return year in and year out to the native rivers in which they were born and enhances the chances of sportsman to catch one on a fly. The local economies in the remote, rural territories where these 'silver swimmers' swim rely on fly fisherman to sustain much of their livelihoods. Without Orri's tenaciousness, wisdom and love for his natural world in Iceland, millions of native salmon would have been killed. How many environmental and economic disasters can you think of that were caused by the direct result of man simply seeking to catch, gather and profit from everything in his grasp in the fastest, most efficient manner possible? Sportsman desire and fight for sustainable harvesting of all native fish and game species. Their dollars support such efforts. The Atlantic Salmon Association (ASF) continues with its steadfast research and monitoring of salmon runs in all the major salmon rivers of the northeastern portion of the United States and Canada. They continue with their efforts for promoting 'catch and release'. They are collecting information on the migratory instincts of the Atlantic salmon from the Northeast coastal sanctuaries up to Greenland. The more we know about the what, why, when and where of salmon movements and behaviors, the more measures we can implement in our quest to save these magnificent fish.

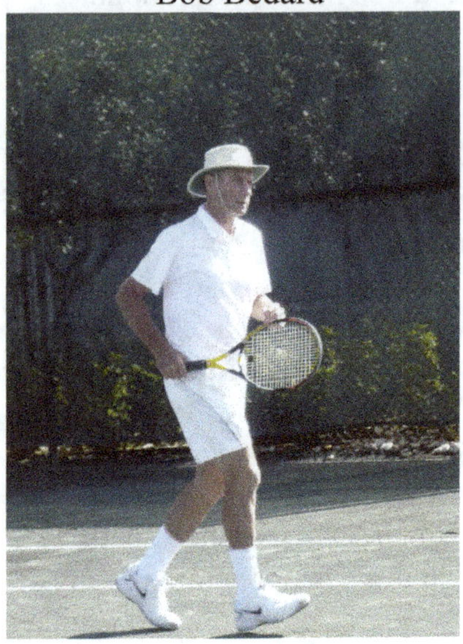
Bob Bedard

I have many sporting interests and tennis has been a major part of my being and physical fitness regime since a boy. Hence it has to fit somewhere in this narrative. Many people complain about the exorbitant salaries paid to professional sport's athletes. It was not too long ago when the best athletes were paid meager salaries with no future monetary guarantees. This was particularly true in the sport of tennis prior to the 'open era,' which began in 1968. Tennis guru Jack Kramer formed a nucleus of the best tennis stars including Tony Trabert, Rod Laver, Roy Emerson, Ken Rosewall, Pancho Gonzales, Lew Hoad and others to bring about professional tennis. These men paved the way so that players could be paid for their talents based on their world rankings. Billy Jean King helped move the women's game forward in much the same way. All of these people and many others not mentioned are true legends of the game.

When I have to focus on one individual, however, the name Robert Bedard comes up front and center. Maybe this is because Bob is a friend of mine who shares the tennis courts with me every winter in Florida. More importantly Bob was Canada's top ranked player for an amazing 10 consecutive years (1955-1965), as well as a member of the Canadian Davis Cup team from 1953-1961 and again in 1967 at the ripe age of 35. He was one of the few Canadians of his time to star on the international tennis scene before the open era. In talking with him recently he told me that his first love was hockey and that he played for five different teams in the same year. Although it was likely that he would have been signed by one of the National Hockey Leagues (NHL) professional teams, his parents convinced him to concentrate on his tennis career and education. Over a span of 39 years from 1967 to

1997 Bob was a college teacher and headmaster. When being inducted into Canada's Sport's Hall of Fame in 1996, Bob stated: *"There is no doubt in my mind that the upward trajectory of my career as an educator has been the result of qualities of an abstract nature which sports inspired in me – discipline, concentration, will, and consistency."* Bob equates athletics with the development of acquired life-skills. He played and succeeded during a time of little monetary gain for his talents and time spent on the courts. In a sense the reality of having to earn a living turned out to be a blessing. As a teacher, his exuberance, intelligence and example in the classroom helped propel his students to a higher understanding of living, scholarship, and duty.

Bob is now 84 years old, and the story isn't over. Far from it. Certainly he made a great difference in the lives he touched over the course of his tennis career and the students that he taught and mentored. What amazes me more today is his extraordinary physical condition, intelligence and running ability on the court. I would say without the blink of an eye that Bob is one of the best-conditioned athletes of his age, and I know of no other tennis player near his age who can do what he can do on the tennis court. He is the best example I can point to of a world-class athlete who has maintained their fitness level, agility and competitiveness in a sport that they have played for over 70 years. To watch him move, hit and beat good players 30 years his junior is simply amazing. Even at his advanced age, his mind and body have been overly-conditioned to think young and to live life to its fullest. Bob winters in Florida with his lovely wife Anne who makes sure he is well-fed and rested before venturing on the court. As Bob told me, *"The reason I have been as good as I am can be directly related to the love and care that Ann has given me over these many years."*

During the great tennis years of the 1950s and 1960s with a much smaller number of super stars than we have today, Bob Bedard held his own against the world's best. Just for nostalgia's sake, many sport history buffs believe that Australian's Rod Laver, Ken Rosewall or Roy Emerson were the best players of their era. Bob played against all of them. But, Bob's toughest foe faced during those years was Lew Hoad, another Australian who is a less-heralded, former world number one who beat Bob several times at various tournaments. Today Bob still plays tennis several times each week and organizes a team at his condo community which plays various teams up and down the Florida coast. When I first met Bob he welcomed me and set up some tennis dates with the local gang of players. He does a great job in his candid, unassuming way of trying to include everyone regardless of ability. It's the teacher in him. Today, probably more importantly than any time in history, young people need good examples to look up to. Bob is one of those examples who gave his all as a teacher, mentor and athlete, and who continues in this realm of excellence even into his eighties. He is a great inspiration to us all. Maybe I can inspire him to fish with me soon.

The world's best-known and accomplished brook trout taxidermist and restorer is 83 year-old David Footer. In viewing his trout, salmon, pike and other fish mounts, I would have to rank him number one overall. His pedigree is unequalled. Learning his trade from Maine's 1930s to 1970s Renaissance man Herbie Welch, Dave has mounted over 6000 fish spanning 60 years. Approximately 75% of these are brook trout. Dave's understanding of wood, metal and various composites coupled with an innate artistic ability and an eye to applying new methods, has greatly improved the quality and longevity of mounts since the Herbie Welch days. His artist's eye skillfully reproduces the fish's scale-colored markings, so that the finished mount looks like it was just caught. What especially sets Dave apart from the pack is his astute understanding and application of real-life colors that are applied once the basic fish profile is ready. They are spectacular pieces of art. His pen and brush-painted wildlife art and illustrations have also received wide acclaim and have been viewed in many publications.

Growing up on the family farm in Lewiston, Maine, Dave developed an affinity for the outdoors at an early age—haying the fields, trapping game along the creek and fishing with his dad. He spent 26 summers guiding on the famous Broadback River in the deep woods of Ontario, and many of his earliest mounts originated from this river. His dutiful assistant and wife Polly passed away recently. Dave and his lovely daughter Julie cared and provided for Polly over several years in their home, not wanting her to be relocated to a nursing facility. I first met Dave in 2008 after returning from a successful fishing trip in northern Quebec. He immediately struck me as a warm, congenial and engaging person as he invited me in his home to see his paintings, wood carvings and taxidermy work. You could sense he was a proud man, and he had a glee in his eye knowing that his work was coveted in fly fishing circles. I would converse with Dave for two years as he prepared and mounted my trophies. Picking up my fish in early spring, 2011, I asked him if he would like to show his work at the 'Arts In The Barn' in Cushing, Maine. He agreed, and the weekend was a great success. The best part for me was watching Dave draw in, converse and explain every piece of art to each person who came to see his work over the course of the day. Where did he get the energy to do this at his age? He repeated each detail at length to each visitor and told them stories about his life and the significance of each painting or mount. His pleasing, welcoming personality and youthful exuberance was self-evident—traits of a man still on a mission and with a passion for life.

"This is a painting I gave to Polly at our anniversary a few years ago. It shows us walking along a glade with our fly rods after an afternoon of fishing on the Salmon

River, New York. By gorry, I have so many fond memories and life has been a blessing to me. Anyways, I love sharing my art and adventures with people and how much this life means to me-by gory I'm a lucky guy. Anyways…………"

ARTS IN THE BARN

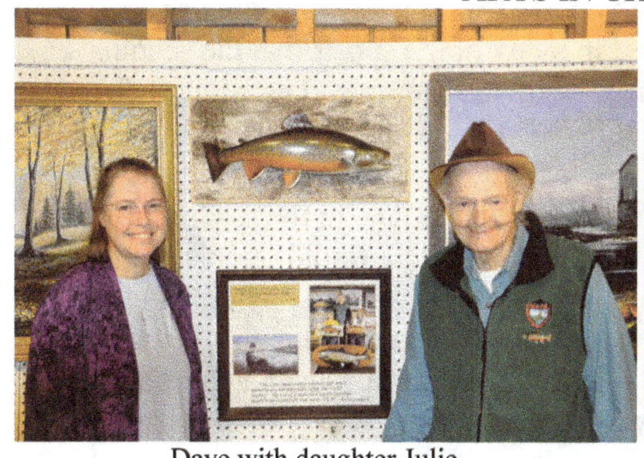

Dave with daughter Julie

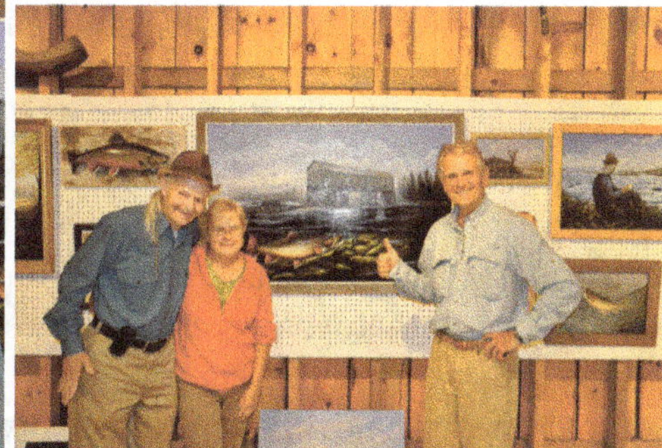

Dave, Pam and Tom

Dave has been generous with his donations of art to worthy charitable causes including those given to the native Crete people of northern Labrador. He has helped and supported many conservation and preservation programs over the course of his life, and has been honored as a recipient of the 'Award of Merit' and 'Certificate of Appreciation' from the 'Hooked on Fishing, Not On Drugs' program of the Department of Inland Fisheries and Maine Warden Service. Many plaques hang on his walls in recognition of his donations and time given to initiatives that help save and promote our natural resources and the wildlife that these resources sustain. Dave never forgot his Maine roots that have helped to keep him humble in a world that has elevated him to a living legend status. But, his legend has been cut, grounded and re-rooted more from a deep desire to communicate the joy of promoting a positive stance to living life to its fullest and serving mankind benevolently.

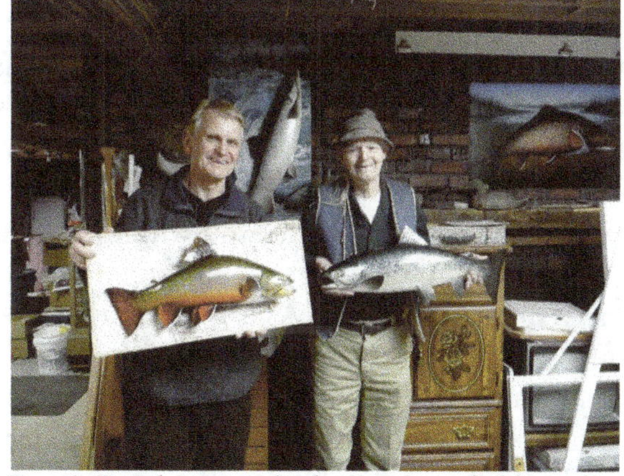

Dave's Brook trout and salmon mounts in his studio

Chapter 18

Food For Thought

For some innate reason I grew up with an eye towards making exercise an important aspect of my life. I participated in many of the sports that the schools provided and was drawn to those that gave the highest aerobic experience such as running, hockey and tennis. At a very young age I knew that God had blessed me with athletic ability. I was fast, quick and felt comfortable in every sport. In between team meets in high school and college, I would take to the roads and typically run 5-10 miles several times a week to keep fit. I would often comment on how well this regimen made me feel, function and think. I felt a physical and mental burst of energy that would carry me throughout the day, coupled with a heightened ability to think, learn and communicate. Untamed stress was never a part of my life. Neuroscience can now better explain my experiences, but I didn't need science to realize the benefits that I was administering to myself beginning in grade school to the present day. There is no question that I would not have been as successful and creative in the business world without a thorough inoculation of physical exercise in my weekly regimen. I'm not alone in this discussion. There are thousands of athletes that can verify similar results. However, many kids are shy and reticent, not athletically inclined and feel alienated from sport's programs that focus only on the motivated athlete. Can these students learn and adapt to incorporate a fitness regimen in their weekly activities if left to fodder on their own? Not likely.

Statistics show us that fewer Americans are hunting and participating in other energetic out-of-door activities, and that this reduction mirrors a growing physically unhealthy population. This reduction in sportsmen weighs heavily on the fiscal vitality of fish and game departments and hurts local economies, conservation initiatives and sporting lodges that rely on the income generated. For example, in the state of Maine, the number of hunters from 1995 to 2009 has dropped 39% for residents and 60% for non-residents who opt for a big game license. Although these statistics are also influenced by other factors, such as how well a state attracts sportsmen through advertising and the complexity of game laws and fees on the books compared to other states, it appears that not as many individuals desire the effort and physical exercise that goes hand-in-hand with the sport. Fishing licenses have seen some increase, but not to the numbers that are needed to sustain a viable and optimum long-term fisheries program. As a sports-minded person, I would like to see sporting programs flourish. I would like to see fish and game departments being fiscally well-funded and managed to optimize the myriad of outdoor experiences for sportsmen. Lastly, I would like to see a healthier population that could enjoy the physical activity that hunting and fishing provides. Since the subject of fitness is a matter that is extremely important and is often overlooked in contemporary America, it needs some attention here.

What is America's state of fitness? It is estimated that by the year 2020 every three out of four Americans will be obese. We are the most unfit nation on the planet. Americans consume foods that contain on average 40% saturated fat (health conscious diets should contain fat levels of 20% or less). Worst yet, we are becoming a country of 'couch and computer-game potatoes' with a lifestyle that can only grow our girths and health care costs. I can't quite fathom all of this. I'm puzzled why our primary and secondary schools are not mandated to teach life-saving nutritional and exercise skills to help with maintaining a healthy population of Americans. The federal and state government direct minimum levels of academic achievement that must be attained and maintained in order for schools to keep their accreditation. But what good are math, science and language skills long-term when they are administered to a growing unhealthy student body? America's position and power in the world of business, politics and education will not just improve with our government's needed initiatives in revitalizing and revamping aptitude tests, tax laws, regulations and other economic resolutions. Our role and position in the world will also weigh heavily on whether Americans can discover, incorporate and maintain healthy living lifestyles.

We could learn much by emulating some of the smaller European countries lifestyles such as Denmark, Austria, Sweden and Switzerland, where physical fitness is more entwined within people's everyday lives. The obesity percentages by population range in the 8 to 9% for these countries. Japan and South Korea have even lower 3% rates. The percentage of Americans grossly overweight is over 30% — a dismal number. I attribute the health of these European and Eastern countries to the early learned benefits of exercise, educated eating habits, and life experiences that value vacation and family time. The Asian countries acquire their lean bodies primarily from their diets rich in low-fat foods which include many vegetables and fish. An important component of European life is that, although many value work and material success, they do not make it their primary focus and reason for living. Much more emphasis is placed on time to enjoy the out-of-doors and their families, resulting in more satisfied lives and less stressful living. There is also strong evidence that Europeans are better prepared for the working world. Overall 40 to 50% of European kids are involved with programs that link the classroom with real-life work programs—thereby tying education with vocation. Upwards of 25% of American kids drop out of high school and this can be directly linked to boredom. Young people need to know the reason behind what they are learning. If they see no reason, their interest wanes and they either do poorly, or they simply drop out. The statistics get worse in college where attrition rates have reached 50%. Apart from the positive health-oriented life styles that exist in Europe, many European governments are experiencing severe monetary problems. They have slowly learned that they need to change many of their social and economic policies that have put them in debt. Many have huge deficits that have plagued them for decades, and now have reached the breaking point. Much of the same can be said about American policies, regulations and politics that plague us here. Governments can help minimize stress and financial worries by decreasing the tax loads and regulations imposed on its citizens, and by doing so, help fuel freedoms that create more robust and creative people. When people feel in control of their lives, they allocate more time for healthy, recreational pursuits.

Our countries greatest resource lies with teaching and our educators. From kindergarten through high school, teachers are the most involved in molding and influencing our population, and they deserve our highest respect, support and praise. But, in order to better educate, they need the tools, freedom and cooperation that is necessary to change their classrooms and schools around for the better. Educators also must find better ways to work with and engage the students with community leaders who would be willing to donate their time to teach kids life-skills required for success in the business and civic world. Fundamentally, one major key to success will involve the linking of learning with real-life experiences in problem-solving group discussions.

Many studies have shown that a fit body helps maintain a fit mind and state of being. A fit mind makes better decisions, and better judgments ultimately make a country more vital, secure and prosperous—particularly when lives are vigorously lengthened with fewer medical complications and health care costs. Of course bad habits and addictions such as smoking and the consumption of too much alcohol will skew the ability of a nation to attain maximum health gains. Much of this behavior could be alleviated once tried and true fitness programs are initiated. Politicians, school districts, and the medical field need to work more closely to educate the general public about the importance of eating more nutritionally valued foods. In conjunction with improving diets, the benefits of starting and maintaining an exercise regimen needs equal focus. Although there are medical, mental and psychological reasons for obesity and other ailments that need addressing at an individual level, much of it unfortunately can be blamed on simple laziness and slothfulness. Too many people have no pride in their appearance, their internal health or are even aware of their dilemma. Too many are soft of body because they are soft with their understanding of what it means to achieve true, meaningful success in life. Optimum success and satisfaction can't be attained unless there is a deliberate attempt to improve one's mind, body and spirit. It takes some get up and go and a burning desire to optimize one's life.

Proper educational initiatives coupled with hands-on community involvement are the keys to lifting people out of their physical, economic and mental poverties. Learning good habits need to begin at an early age. The good news is that we can institute programs that have already proven highly successful at several of our American public schools. Naperville Central High School in Naperville, Illinois has successfully instituted a physical fitness program that has dramatically increased their student's ability to learn.

They are teaching fitness and lifestyle skills (not sports per se), and blending it in with academic excellence. In this age of 'Leave No Child Behind' where academic testing has taken precedence over 'free-time', recess-time and physical fitness time, our children are being stressed in an atmosphere that does not allow for 'down time' and physical activity. Multiple studies have shown clearly that when physical exercise is blended with academic learning, students significantly improve their test scores, are happier and are noticeably better adjusted in their social interactions. Neuroscientists have discovered that aerobic exercise stimulates the brain to a heightened position of cognitive function and learning ability. So why do only 6% of U.S. high schools offer a daily physical education class? Is it because it would mandate a major change in focus and force changes that could take most schools out of their comfort zones? Is it because course structure and testing procedures have left no time for physical fitness? With the solid evidence at hand, all educators must begin to equate aerobic exercise with better functioning brains and higher test scores. Today there is simply no excuse for any further 'leadership laziness' by not implementing tried and true physical fitness programs in all our schools.

A book that I highly recommend and which should be mandatory reading for all academic and administrative leaders is *Spark: The Revolutionary New Science of Exercise and the Brain* by Dr. John J. Ratey and Eric Hagerman. This book is a must read for those implementing and re-designing school curriculums to accommodate a physical fitness schedule. Education is expensive. Let's maximize our tax dollars and make fit leaders and thinkers to guide America into the 21st century and beyond.

"Common sense is not so common."

~ Voltaire

Eating Nature-ally

We hear more about the benefits of 'natural foods' and the reasons to avoid corn-fed, steroid/growth hormone-injected animal meat and vegetables and fruits that have been sprayed with pesticides. Although Pam and I are not fanatics when it comes to reading every label and micro-managing every meal, we are aware of the major benefits of blending a variety of food types and exercising the body and brain on a regular basis. This year our modest garden provided us with apples, pears, tomatoes, swiss chard, rhubarb and a variety of squashes — true organic foods. Maintaining strength and fitness can't be accomplished with poor nutritional choices. Consuming good foods helps to foster more enjoyable and energetic lives. Hiking, fishing, hunting and all outdoor activities are enhanced when the mind and body are conditioned and ready for action. However, it is important to be aware that much of what is advertised as 'natural' isn't necessarily natural at all, and even if touted as 'organic' may not render any more nutritional value than cheaper competitive brands. Marketing plays an important role in what we purchase and the consumer must use discernment and logic to weed out deceitful labeling and false claims. For example, Americans spent over $80 billion in 2010 for their yearly growing desire for seafood. According to a recent Consumer's Report study, it was found that 25 to 30 % of seafood is mislabeled in the world marketplace. Not surprising, the consumer was deceived into paying higher prices for inferior or more cheaply produced fish. Health issues are paramount here as well. One sample that Consumer Reports tested was labeled as grouper, only to find that it was actually tilefish which contain three times more mercury as grouper. The Food and Drug Administration warns women of childbearing age and children to avoid tilefish entirely.
Although federal law requires seafood to be labeled truthfully, the FDA which oversees labeling relinquishes much of its responsibilities to state and local agencies. State officials acknowledge that their inspectors are mostly trained to cover food safety issues — not educated to have knowledge about all the various fish species. Since we, the consumer, are left to fodder for ourselves, wouldn't it be best if we all became 'natural gatherers' (gardeners, fisherman and hunters) so that we would know what we were actually eating? If done in enough numbers we could significantly help reduce the exploitation of endangered fish species such as Atlantic salmon and blue fin tuna by decreasing the overall demand. Yes, I'm being more than facetious here. I don't actually believe that this would ever happen in the numbers needed for recovery, but I dream like it could. And this comes from the mouth of a pragmatist who has spent his lifetime building a business, and who is a strong believer and proponent of a stronger capitalistic-based enterprise system. A century ago we were indeed a country of 'gatherers'. Since we are now unfortunately a country of more 'takers' than 'providers', there will be only so much we can do to reverse the tide. But, trying to reverse the tide is in the best interest of

us all. The gist from much of this discussion is that, above all else, we must strive to gain these kinds of independence, health and additional freedoms in an imperfect world. By doing so, we might help relieve the burden that we bare upon the earth's natural resources.

As we continue to push and legislate for cleaner rivers, streams and oceans, mercury and other forms of carcinogens and poisons will hopefully become less of a concern to us. Fish, particularly those with high levels of omega fats like salmon and mackerel are beneficial, particularly if they are 'wild' and not 'farmed raised'. Certain species contain higher levels of mercury than others, and one can find in charts which ones are the healthiest to eat and how often they should be consumed. Natural meats are another matter. Organic meats are not always easy to find, and they are most always very expensive. If possible, it is best to consume the best of the natural meats such as venison, moose, caribou, buffalo and elk. Hunters and non-hunters are beginning to eat more woods-raised or farm-raised venison for its low-fat source of protein, minerals and vitamins—all of which are free from chemicals and human tampering. To put this into some perspective, a 3 and1/2 ounce portion of ground beef has 223% more fat, 40% more calories, and 125% more cholesterol than the same amount of venison.

Orchestrated diets rarely work, yet there are thousands of books promoting one eating method over another, with a society paying billions of dollars each year to find the perfect fix. The more we read, the fatter we get. Specific diet programs most often don't work, and many have proved harmful. It's the person's thought process, upbringing, education, independence and health-oriented habits that we need be focused on. If more Americans demanded healthier foods, these foods would find their way into the markets at less cost. It's my desire to have people enjoy their lives and not jeopardize them with poor habits that increase their medical bills, shorten their lives and put undue stress on their families and our health care system. The task of turning things around is daunting, but the consequences of not addressing and reversing these problems now are catastrophic.

"The greatest wealth is health."

~Virgil

Charlene Anderson's Venison Steak Marinade (mmm…mmm…good)

1/3 cup Lemon Juice, 2 cloves Minced Garlic, 1-1/2 cups Oil,
¾ cup Soy Sauce, ¼ cup Worcestershire Sauce
2 teaspoons dry Mustard, 2 teaspoons Salt, 1 tablespoon black Pepper,
1-1/2 teaspoon Parsley, ½ cup Wine Vinegar
   (Mix generously with 2 lbs meat in plastic bag. Let sit in refrigerator for several hours to overnight.)

Katie Johnson's Succulent Venison Stew

2 lb cut Venison Stew Meat, Carrots or Parsnips, small Red Potatoes,
Spinach or Bok Choy, Zucchini, Mushrooms, 1large Sweet Onion,
7 cups Beef Bouillon (cut vegetables to similar size)

Salt and pepper the meat, sprinkle with flour. Over medium heat, melt 2 tablespoons of butter and 2 tablespoons of vegetable oil in Dutch oven pot. Brown the meat on all sides, and put in bowl when done. In the Dutch oven pot melt 2 tablespoons of butter and 2 tablespoons of vegetable oil. Add cut up onions and mushrooms over medium heat for 5 minutes. Add 3 cloves of garlic (minced) and cook for 3 more minutes.

Add 7 cups of broth and bring to boil. Add in meat with heat at medium high. Add all remaining vegetables to soup pot with 2 good-sized rosemary sprigs and 2 bay leaves. Cover and simmer for 2 hours.

   Venison steaks, loins and wild game in general are low in fat and hence fry or broil quickly. The best results for rare to medium cooked meat is to prepare it over high heat for a short time; test with a knife to check the desired redness while cooking. When dressing my own deer or having a butcher prepare my cuts, I specify one-inch thickness where ever possible. Four to five minutes on each side usually does the trick. When the cuts are too thin they tend to get too well done quickly and have a tendency to taste dry. In the attempt to retain the meat's juices and nutrients it's always best to have thicker sections. Sautéed onions and mushrooms always complement the meat nicely. If time or lack of ingredients prevent you from making a marinade, simply fry or grill wild game in olive oil with a dash of pepper and salt at relatively high heat. I personally like my venison alongside homemade baked beans and a garden salad—great tasting and satisfying natural nutrition at its finest.

Who Belongs

The rock lies silently upon the hill, the tree whistles with the wind,
the country brook echoes its song against the mountain rim.

The distant sky is filled with pearls, the moon makes shadows out of hills,
the owl flies quietly until it kills with shrills.

The lowly rill reflects nature's still, unmoving in the night.
What is it that brings me here to gaze upon this lonesome fear?

Lights are low at distant homes, there are no other birds that fly.
Why do I come to this familiar place with no light but that of the skies?

I must commune with nature, to hear trout rising to the hatch, but it is getting late.
My eyes want to dose and leave this world to those more suitable for the day's close.

I stay to listen and stare as nature lays with me here, alone, I feel the earth's pulse
with senses on high alert in a heart that conceals the most.

Another sound approaches near — it is a deer with young to rear coming to drink of
brook so clear, those waters of my first catching trout.

It is their life tonight, not mine. It is their kingdom on which I tread.
Even the stately woodchuck yonder knows that I, an alien, should be in bed.

And so I leave this world to them, the owners of its entire,
as I go off with secret thoughts to retire.

Author

NOTES